COMMUN

FOR INTERNATIONAL

BUSINESS

D1650652

THE SECRETS OF

EXCELLENT

INTERPERSONAL SKILLS

BOB   ter

Collins

HarperCollins Publishers
77-85 Fulham Palace Road
Hammersmith
London W6 8JB

First edition 2013

Reprint 10 9 8 7 6 5 4 3 2 1 0

© 2013 York Associates

ISBN 978-0-00-749958-8

www.collinslanguage.com

A catalogue record for this book is available from the British Library

Typeset in India by Aptara

Printed and bound in Great Britain by Clays Ltd, St Ives plc

Collins

COMMUNICATION
FOR INTERNATIONAL
BUSINESS

THE SECRETS OF
EXCELLENT
INTERPERSONAL SKILLS

ABOUT THE AUTHORS

Bob Dignen is a director of York Associates. He specialises in international competence development, delivering international team seminars to clients across Europe. He also coaches project leaders operating across cultures, facilitates project meetings and runs international team-building sessions. His published titles include *Managing Projects* (Delta Publishing), *Communicating Across Cultures* (Cambridge University Press), *Communicating Internationally in English* (York Associates), *50 Ways to Improve Your Presentation Skills* and *50 Ways to Improve Your Intercultural Skills* (Summertown, Cengage). He is also co-author of *Developing People Internationally*, a multimedia international team training resource developed by York Associates.

Ian McMaster has been editor-in-chief of the bi-monthly business English magazine *Business Spotlight* since it was launched in 2001. He was also editor-in-chief of the general English magazine *Spotlight* from 1995 to 2003 and from 2006 to 2009. His specialist research interest is the use of English as a lingua franca in business, and communication problems between native and non-native speakers.

ABOUT YORK ASSOCIATES

The mission of York Associates is to develop people internationally. For the last thirty years, it has been helping people who work internationally to get results by helping them to communicate effectively across language and cultural boundaries. The company offers a range of training in international leadership, intercultural, communication and language skills to private and public sector clients worldwide. It has a training centre in York in the UK that delivers English and international communication training mainly to non-native professionals, while most of its international team and leadership training takes place at client premises. York Associates is also a publisher of innovative titles in the field of international communication.

ABOUT BUSINESS SPOTLIGHT

This book has been developed and published in association with *Business Spotlight*, a bi-monthly business English magazine aimed primarily at German speakers who need English in their jobs.

THANKS

The authors would like to thank Will Capel for his editorial support; Steve Flinders, York Associates director, for editing the original title on which this book is based; Mike Seymour of Corporate Language Training (Cologne) for his collaboration on the online survey carried out in 2009 together with *Business Spotlight*, York Associates and Zurich Academy in Europe, which contributed to the thinking underlying the original title; and *Business Spotlight* magazine for its ongoing support for this project.

CONTENTS

INTRODUCTION

WHO IS THIS BOOK FOR?

Communication for International Business has been written for professionals who wish to become better international communicators at work.

THE BENEFITS OF THIS BOOK

The aim of the book is to help you to develop your international communication skills. It will develop your ability to get your message across more clearly and persuasively in a range of international contexts.

It will help you to use forms of English which are more understandable for your non-native speaking colleagues, who frequently struggle to follow native speakers in professional contexts. Native speaker English is often over-complex, spoken too quickly, and full of confusing vocabulary and abbreviations. This book will help you to communicate in English more clearly and respectfully with others.

The book will also make you more mindful of intercultural differences, and help you to think about how best to adapt your communication style to specific individuals in specific situations.

The first part of the book, The basics, will enable you to get your message across more clearly when speaking. It will also help you to listen in ways that will create better understanding with international colleagues and business partners.

In the second part of the book, Face-to-face skills, we give you ideas on how to improve core business communication skills – building relationships, networking, influencing, making decisions, managing conflict and building trust.

The third part, Virtual skills, looks at different aspects of virtual communication, including advice on how to write better emails, how to manage conference calls, and ways to be effective in international virtual teams.

In addition, there are four case studies which appear at intervals through the book and a reading list at the back of the book.

INTERNATIONAL COMMUNICATION IS SITUATIONAL

The problem with giving advice about international communication is that it often ends up coming down to 'Well, it depends on the situation.' In fact, it is extremely difficult (and dangerous) to list absolute dos and don'ts for you to apply across all cultural contexts in all international business contexts. That is simply unrealistic.

What you will take away from this book is a stronger realisation that if you want to become a successful international communicator, you need to reflect regularly as to how you communicate and what you communicate. You will think more about how you need to adapt your message and the way you communicate, even the words you are using and how quickly you speak, according to the people you are talking to in each specific situation. Each one has three main elements:

1 Culture

Think about the values, behaviours and communication styles that you are likely to meet in each different international situation. Try to understand the different attitudes, for example to deadlines, to leadership, to teamwork, to decision-making, to relationships and to hierarchy, which shape how people communicate. It is not only national cultural differences which can have an impact on your chances of successful communication. Organisational culture, professional culture and other layers of culture can also be significant. When you have analysed the cultural context in which you are working, then you can decide how much you need to adapt your own communication style to that context.

2 Person

Consider the unique individual(s) in front of you. Cultural knowledge gives you only very general information about attitudes and behaviours. But we never communicate with cultures, we only communicate with individuals. As an international communicator, listen to people carefully and try to understand the specific personalities of the people you work with. Then you can adapt your communication style and strategy appropriately to the individual as appropriate.

3 Business context

Professional people work to get results. The business context may lead us to cooperate with some people, but may put us into conflict with others, so skills like influencing and managing conflict are also essential when we work internationally. We always have to think about the business environment when we choose our communication strategy. What is the organisation trying to achieve? What roles do people have? What are the barriers to cooperation? How can we balance our interests against those of others? At York Associates, we call this 'achieving results through relationships'.

This book is primarily written for people communicating in English for business internationally. However, I have been told that my training is not limited to the international or intercultural arena but has more universal inter-human value. In other words, you will also be able to apply many of the ideas and approaches in this book in your own domestic contexts, in private as well as in business, with family as well as with colleagues and customers.

ABOUT THIS EDITION

Communication for International Business is based on *Communicating Internationally in Business*, which was published by York Associates in association with *Business Spotlight* in 2011. This edition has been rewritten to support the particular communication needs of native speakers working internationally.

Note: The authors are aware that the terms *native speaker* (NS) and *non-native speaker* (NNS) are not entirely satisfactory in relation to English. Many people cannot easily be put into one or other or these categories, for example because they have grown up in multilingual families or societies. The term 'non-native speaker' is also sometimes regarded as derogatory. This is not the authors' intention, and despite the problematic nature of the terms, we believe that they are still a useful approximation in many international contexts.

FEEDBACK

Good international communicators always ask for feedback. So please let us know your thoughts, whether positive or negative, after reading this book. We want to learn from you too, so we look forward to hearing from you.

Bob Dignen

1

USING ENGLISH FOR INTERNATIONAL COMMUNICATION

'In my opinion, native speakers often use their language as a weapon.

E.S., senior German international insurance executive, during a training course

If you work internationally, you will have to communicate with both native and non-native speakers of English in your meetings, negotiations, presentations and when socialising.

Native and non-native speakers of English can cause communication problems for each other. The native speaker may find the non-native speaker difficult to understand because of his/her accent, choice of vocabulary or non-standard grammar. But more importantly the non-native speaker may struggle with what the native speaker is saying because the latter is not adapting his/her speaking style and language level adequately and appropriately to the situation. Indeed, as the quotation above suggests, native speakers may be seen to be using their advantage with English to dominate meetings, conference calls and other business situations with consequences that do not have a positive business outcome from the perspective of their non-native speaker colleagues.

In this chapter we report on the results of some research into native and non-native speaker communication in English, and provide guidelines for how you can improve your international communication style.

Before you read on, think about these questions:

1. What can make native speakers difficult to understand?

2. What problems do you have when communicating with non-native speakers of English?

3. How can native speakers make themselves easier to understand?

In 2007 more than 1,000 German-speaking users of English at work took part in a survey for *Business Spotlight*, a magazine for German professionals who want to improve their English language and communication skills. They came from all industries, sizes of companies and departments, and from all levels of the corporate ladder. Just under half said that English is one of the official languages in their firms.

This chapter reports on the results of this survey and the implications for how you need to communicate internationally.

COMMUNICATION TASKS OF NON-NATIVE SPEAKERS

The survey first set out to discover what tasks non-native speakers are most likely to have to perform in English at work. The main tasks that this group had to perform regularly in English are shown in Table 1 (see page 15).

Emails top the list, followed by telephoning. 33 per cent of all respondents said they took part in meetings regularly and 22 per cent had to negotiate. Just 14 per cent said they have to give presentations often or very often in English, but twice as many had to listen to such talks. The table also shows the importance of small talk and socialising, skills that are essential for developing relationships and networking.

How does this data help native speakers to be more effective international communicators? Firstly, the fact that email is top of the

TABLE 1: Which tasks do you perform often or very often at work in English?	
Reading emails	72%
Writing emails	67%
Telephoning	55%
Reading letters	53%
Reading job-specific literature	49%
Writing letters	46%
Making small talk	45%
Socialising	40%

Source: *Business Spotlight* Survey, 2007.

list, and is more important than telephoning, for example, correlates with the message from many non-native speakers that they generally prefer to write and read rather than speak and listen: writing and reading allow more time to construct and decode messages in a foreign language. A key competence for native speakers is, therefore, to be able to write clear and simple English. They should also use written communication frequently to prepare for and summarise face-to-face and virtual meetings and telephone calls.

It is interesting that negotiations and, particularly, presentations are less frequently part of working life. A lower frequency means less practice, resulting in these two communication tasks being perceived as more challenging. Negotiating requires thinking on one's feet, and having to find convincing arguments or respond to new ideas quickly. Presenting is demanding because it means extended and very public exposure in the foreign language. Native speakers, as communication partners in these situations, either as negotiating counterparts or as a presentation audience, need to make allowances for the added complexity of these tasks for international colleagues and customers.

Finally, on small talk and socialising, associated research indicates that this is the communication area that the largest proportion of respondents had problems with. This is important because many native speakers, as they recount stories and fire off well-intended questions about the political system or sporting interests of their counterparts, may not realise how challenging small talk is. Very often non-native speakers feel uncomfortable because they lack the vocabulary to talk about a wide range of topics in depth. For the native speaker, keeping things simple – not going into too much detail, not telling too many stories and not invoking too many cultural references – is essential to keep things engaging for international partners.

COMMUNICATION PROBLEMS

The survey asked about the communication problems between native and non-native speakers. While 39 per cent of respondents said that they found other non-native speakers easier to understand, 24 per cent – mainly those with better language skills – found it is easier to communicate with native speakers.

TABLE 2: Which factors cause communication problems for you in English at work?		
	With native speakers	With non-native speakers
They speak too fast.	86%	10%
They use unknown expressions.	60%	10%
They use too much idiomatic language.	57%	3%
They use difficult words.	56%	11%
They do not speak clearly enough.	56%	61%
They have a heavy accent.	45%	58%
I cannot make myself understood.	16%	24%
They talk too much.	13%	5%
They make grammar mistakes.	2%	53%

Source: *Business Spotlight* Survey, 2007.

As Table 2 shows (see page 16), the main complaints about native speakers were that they talk too quickly and use unknown words and expressions and too much idiomatic language. Lower language-level non-native speakers have particular problems with business partners who speak too fast. Other problems with native speakers include not speaking clearly (mumbling or articulating poorly) and having strong accents.

A later online survey in 2009 – carried out jointly by *Business Spotlight*, Corporate Language Training (Cologne), York Associates and Zurich Academy in Europe – looked specifically at the problems that non-native speakers experience in telephone conference calls. It found very similar results, as well as problems caused by native speakers using unknown abbreviations, not giving enough opportunities for non-native speakers to clarify what they mean, and speaking too quietly. These survey results are invaluable for native speakers because they point both to the types of behaviour they need to avoid when communicating internationally and, more implicitly, to the behaviour to aspire to.

TABLE 3: I have problems making English native speakers understand me because ...	
my vocabulary is too limited.	52%
I find it difficult to interrupt discussions to give an opinion.	41%
English native speakers do not ask questions to clarify what I have said.	26%
the conference calls are not well facilitated.	18%
my limited command of grammar means my English is not clear enough.	14%
my communication style is not clear for them.	11%
native English speakers interrupt me before I have finished.	9%
my pronunciation accent is unclear.	7%

Source: *Business Spotlight* et al, Survey, 2009.

In this survey, in which 164 German speakers took part, we also asked non-native speakers why they thought they had problems making English native speakers understand them. The results are shown in Table 3 (see page 17).

Clearly, many non-native speakers feel that their limited vocabulary – and, to a lesser extent, their limited grammar – is the key problem. In many cases, this may certainly be so. Yet observation of conference calls shows that problems caused by a lack of communication competences – for example, poor listening skills or a failure to clarify – are often equally important. One example in the findings is that many people, particularly women, find it difficult to interrupt discussions and thus manage the communication process.

This data has implications for the communication strategies which native speakers should employ in international meetings:

1 Support people to express their ideas

Survey respondents reported that they feel their vocabulary and grammar is limited. In other words, what they are saying is not actually what they ideally want to say. This means native speakers need to support others to express themselves, perhaps by clarifying, paraphrasing, or even networking before meetings, to find out what people want to say and then saying it for them.

2 Involve people in discussions

The difficulty expressed with interruption is another interesting statistic. It means non-native speakers may be quieter than they want to be; they may be participating less and not at the most opportune moments because they cannot 'get a word in edgeways'. What does this mean for the native speaker? It means inviting audience members more often to comment on what has been said (to facilitate interruption). It probably also means talking in shorter segments – perhaps bursts of ninety seconds and not five minutes – before handing over.

3 Rotate facilitation

Think about who facilitates your international meetings. It might be useful to give the role to a non-native speaker as their pace may be more suited to the international audience.

TABLE 4: I use the following strategies often or very often.	
Understanding	
I ask the speaker to clarify what he/she said.	37%
I ask the speaker to slow down.	17%
I ask the meeting leader to tell the English native speakers to speak clearly.	3%
Speaking	
I ask people to confirm that they have understood what I said.	34%
I ask other participants to help me explain my ideas clearly.	17%
I repeat my message until everyone understands.	9%

Source: *Business Spotlight* et al, Survey, 2009.

4 Be patient

Nine per cent of respondents report that they are interrupted by native speakers before they have finished speaking. This suggests that a little patience may be useful, simply allowing an individual the time needed to get their ideas on the table. Without this basic attitude of respect, trust-based international cooperation may prove difficult to achieve.

The survey also asked about the strategies that non-native speakers use to manage the communication process (see Table 4). The results show that non-native speakers seem to be under-using these communication strategies.

The implication for native speakers is twofold

1. Native speakers need to employ these very same strategies towards other native speakers, to help everyone around the table understand and participate. This might result in the unusual situation of a native speaker participant asking for clarification when he/she already understands what has been said. But the clarification is intended to make sure it is clear for everyone else.

2. Native speakers who are leaders of international teams need to coach non-native speakers to use these communication strategies, to build individual competence and communicative effectiveness.

GUIDELINES FOR NATIVE SPEAKERS

Here are some key tips on how you can improve the communication process.

Slow down and stay slowed down. Most native speakers talk too quickly for their non-native colleagues. You need to slow down and concentrate on keeping your speed down. Too often, native speakers slow down for a couple of minutes when asked, but then speed up again. Native speakers need to be alert to the value of pausing more.

Speak clearly. Native speakers need to articulate words more precisely – perhaps over-precisely – to help their international colleagues. For example, *going to* is clearer than *gonna*; and *I will* is clearer than *I'll*. This may sound unnatural to your ear but for the non-native speaker it is likely to be far easier to understand.

Speak more simply. This means using common vocabulary, shorter sentences and simpler grammar; avoiding abbreviations (so *as soon as possible* is better than *asap*, and *managing director* is better than *MD*); and avoiding culturally specific idioms (so *We are in a difficult situation* is better than sporting metaphors such as *We are on a sticky wicket*).

Check understanding. Good international communicators check regularly for understanding, rephrase things that are not clear, and summarise frequently. However, be sensitive to the fact that in some cultures and to some individuals excessive clarification may come across as scepticism or even as a challenge. You may, therefore, need to preface clarification with positive wrappers such as *That sounds interesting/important. You mean that ...*

Use a standard accent. Most non-native speakers of English in Europe will have learned the language from a standard British or American pronunciation model. It can therefore be a challenge to understand a native speaker with a strong national or regional accent. Native speakers should make an effort to move their pronunciation to a more standard model when working internationally.

Speak less. The longer native speakers talk, the more challenging it is for non-native listeners. They should try to say what they want to say in no more than one or two minutes at a time, and then allow others to contribute or clarify.

Be structured and logical. Cultural differences and differences in personality make it difficult to say what is right and wrong, but well-structured and logical inputs are usually easier to understand. For example, using rhetorical markers such as *firstly, secondly, thirdly ...* enable listeners to follow arguments much more easily.

Avoid humour. A lot of humour is very culturally based and can irritate people who are under pressure to understand key information. This may give the feeling that communication becomes rather boring or tedious, without the usual spice and ironic cut-and-thrust banter of the office. At least in the early phases of contact with new international partners, playing it safe like this may be the more effective communication strategy.

Take turns. Native speakers need to invite people to comment on or clarify what they have said. You can use simple questions such as *What do you think?* or *What's your experience in this area?* These inclusive questions are very important to overcome the common perception that native speakers are seeking to achieve an unfair advantage with their language dominance.

Avoid sudden changes of subject. Native speakers need to avoid sudden topic shifts during conference calls, as this can be difficult for non-native speakers to follow. Native speakers need to stay longer on single topics, repeating ideas and giving time for their international colleagues to contribute to the discussion.

Native-to-native: be careful! When native speakers talk to each other, the language gets faster and more complex and often becomes incomprehensible to non-native speakers. So limit native-to-native communication and, if it does happen, make sure the key points are summarised for the rest of the group.

THE NATIVE SPEAKER'S RESPONSIBILITY

If any non-native speaker has not understood what you have said or seems to doubt that you have understood what they have said, then this is your problem as a native speaker and not their problem. You have the flexibility as a speaker to be able to adapt messages to suit different audiences, and to help facilitate diverse groups to build common understanding. This is partly a communicative responsibility but it is also a basic requirement of international leadership. If teams are to achieve high levels of performance, they need international leaders who can express their own ideas clearly and who can enable others to do the same.

2

SPEAKING

*It is impossible to speak in such a way that you
cannot be misunderstood.*

Karl Popper, Austro-British philosopher (1902–94)

Successful communication is a challenge for us all. When we speak,
we have to think a lot about how to get our message across clearly
to others.

In this chapter we look at some of the principles of clear speaking and at some strategies that will help you to communicate more
successfully internationally. You will have the opportunity to profile
your speaking style and identify the factors that may make it difficult
for people to understand you, particularly non-native English speakers. You will also be able to develop a personal development plan to
become a better speaker.

Before you read on, think about these questions:

1. How can I make sure that other people understand what I want to
   say?
2. What kind of communication style do I have? For example, do I
   speak fast or slowly, and do I use long or short sentences?
3. Is there anything in the way that I speak that makes it difficult for
   other people to understand me?
4. How easy is it for non-native speakers of English to understand
   me?

UNDERSTANDING THE SPEAKING CHALLENGE

The quotation from Karl Popper highlights the fact that there is always a communication gap between what speakers say and what listeners understand. This is caused by the process of *interpretation*, as we can see in the classic sender-receiver model of communication:

Interpretation

Communication
Sender speaks   *gap*   Listener 'understands'
message   message

Senders of messages (speakers) need to recognise that whatever they say will be interpreted by receivers (listeners) and therefore can be misunderstood. The risk of misunderstanding is greater when communicating internationally for these language reasons: a word can be wrongly translated, an accent may cause comprehension problems, complex grammar may create confusion, and so on. Cultural differences and aspects of the international environment, poor technology used for a telephone conference, can also lead to communication problems. And a listener's individual personality can always filter and distort what is heard.

As speakers, we need to be sensitive to the unique perspectives of different listeners. We need to know, for example, what they value, what their interests are, what information they can understand, how much English they understand and which forms of communication they see as polite and clear.

TIPS FOR SUCCESSFUL SPEAKING

To be successful, speakers need to communicate the right things in a clear and sensitive way to listeners. So as speakers, we should think carefully about both our own needs *and* the needs of listeners when building and delivering our messages. If we do this, there is a better chance that listeners will:

- understand us
- act on what we say
- be more motivated and more convinced by what we have to say
- feel more trusting toward us.

To be successful, speakers should focus on four main dimensions in their communication, which we can call **TIPS**:

Target
Information
Process
Style

1 TARGET

Problems often occur in international business because people misunderstand the objective behind a message. These misunderstandings can happen even with simple questions such as *Have you finished that report yet?* Is this simply a question to check the status of the report, or is there an underlying push, even a criticism, because the report is overdue?

There is a story of how an employee in Germany completely misinterpreted the meaning of one sentence spoken by his American CEO during a webcast. The CEO finished with this invitation:

If you have any comments on this webcast or about the organisation, please contact me.

The CEO's intention was not to make an invitation to people to give very detailed feedback on the webcast, but more to provide a polite and formulaic ending. But the German employee interpreted this as a serious invitation. He responded by writing a long email detailing what he saw as serious problems in the organisation, including poor communication from the management in his local area. The result was a strong reprimand from his immediate boss, who had received a less than friendly call from the head office in the US. The interpretation was, in fact, a fair one. The underlying intention behind the message was unclear.

> **GOOD PRACTICE 1**
> **State your objective clearly.**
> Here are five key tips to help you to make sure that your international colleagues understand what your objectives are when you talk to them.
>
> **1** Give enough background information so that the listener can interpret your message correctly.
> **2** State your main message in a way that the other sees as positive and polite.
> **3** Use easy-to-understand words and sentences.
> **4** Make it clear what you are *not* talking about in order to avoid misinterpretation.
> **5** Show that you recognise and appreciate the listener's situation.

Be clear, be sensitive

Even when the objective is clear to the speaker, communication can fail if the speaker does not think about the listener's point of view. Speakers often focus too much on their own agendas.

A good example is the way many managers communicate about change. They often communicate the official messages about cost savings but do not talk enough about the fears of those experiencing the change. They should spend more time explaining the impact of the savings on everyday working life and talking through the practical steps that people could take to deal with the changes.

This focus on the listener is one of the keys to successful speaking. Treat listeners as your 'communication customers' and try to find a way to take their needs and expectations into account in your messages.

> **GOOD PRACTICE 2**
> **Adapt the way you express your objective to the listener.**
> Balance your needs as a speaker against those of the listener.

2 INFORMATION

Once speakers are clear about their objectives, the next step is to think carefully about the information to communicate. Listeners may view information in very different ways, according to their cultural background and what they already know. The two key dimensions are what information to communicate, and how extensive and complex this information should be.

Which information?

Successful speakers say things that are relevant to their listeners. If what is said is not relevant, listeners quickly switch off because they cannot see the point of listening.

> **GOOD PRACTICE 3**
> **Select information that is interesting and useful for the listener.**
> Successful speakers talk about things in a way which makes the job of listening easy.

How much information and how complex?

Successful speakers communicate things that are understandable. Otherwise, listeners are likely to become confused and demotivated, and stop listening. This will certainly happen if you give too much information or if your information is too complex. So speakers need to adapt what they say to the preferences, knowledge and competence of their listeners.

> **GOOD PRACTICE 4**
> **K.I.S.S.S.S.**
> One golden rule of good communication is K.I.S.S. (Keep It Short and Simple) but good international communicators go further: they use K.I.S.S.S.S. This means: Keep It …
>
> - Short
> - Simple
> - Structured, and
> - Several times repeated.

CASE STUDY: Getting it wrong

A senior manager in a French bank made a serious communication mistake after his bank took over an important financial institution in an Eastern European country. He travelled there to make a presentation of the French organisation and spent the first morning telling his new colleagues about the proud history and traditions of their new parent company. Why did things go wrong? Because the local managers were feeling insecure about the takeover process, were worried about their jobs, and feared the loss of their own identity and traditions. They were not reassured by a long presentation that seemed to tell them in great detail about how much better and more efficient their new owner was. The speaker went with the wrong objective and communicated the wrong information.

GOOD PRACTICE 5
Communicate the right information and the right amount of information.
Not all information is useful information. Bear in mind the language ability and the professional needs and preferences of different listeners when you choose how much information to give and how complex this information should be. Do not be afraid to repeat key messages. Repetition gives listeners more than one opportunity to hear things, which is particularly important for non-native speakers of English.

3 PROCESS

Communication is a process of interaction between speakers and listeners. This process includes the rules and procedures that people follow in different situations. For example, in one department or organisation, meeting processes might involve starting on time and inviting everyone to summarise their activities since the last meeting. In another department or organisation, meetings might involve waiting for the boss to arrive and then listening to him/her talk at length before anyone else speaks. When people from one meetings culture work with those from another, it can be very useful to agree on a process which suits both parties.

> **GOOD PRACTICE 6**
> **Manage the process as well as the content of communication.**
> Successful speakers use standard expressions to manage the process of typical business communication situations.

Let us look more closely at the process involved in presentations, which can vary greatly between cultures, both national and corporate. Some audiences sit in respectful silence until the speaker has finished; other audiences want to get involved and comment, add their own experiences, and ask lots of questions. And members of other audiences may feel that it is perfectly acceptable to talk to each other while the speaker is talking.

As the speaker, you need to be sensitive to these different expectations. If you are not, you may manage the process in a way that frustrates, irritates or confuses the audience. Good international speakers explicitly negotiate the communication process so that everyone is clear about what is going to happen. Here are some examples of how to do this.

1. Negotiating the question process in a presentation: *Would you prefer to ask questions during the presentation, or shall we leave questions to the end?*
2. Clarifying the place of decision-making in a meeting: *Just to clarify, are we planning to take a decision today, or is this just a preliminary meeting?*
3. Clarifying what is polite to ask in social situations: *Can I ask you about your family? I hope I'm not being rude by asking this, am I?*

According to the INCA (Intercultural Competence Assessment) project, this form of explicit rule management is a key intercultural competence. INCA states that a fully interculturally competent individual 'is able to relate problems of intercultural action to conflicting communication conventions; is able to identify and is ready to adapt to new discourse rules to prevent or clarify misunderstandings'.

> **GOOD PRACTICE 7**
> **When there are different expectations, negotiate an agreed process of communication.**
> The negotiation of a process may sometimes seem time-consuming or even unnecessary. But conflicting expectations can lead to significant misunderstanding, so in the long run, it is worth spending extra time negotiating the process.

Turn-taking principles

In their book *Riding the Waves of Culture: Understanding Cultural Diversity in Business*, Fons Trompenaars and Charles Hampden Turner describe models of turn taking in meetings in different national cultures. The graphic below is a simplified representation of patterns said to be characteristic of different business cultures.

Different patterns of turn taking during meetings

The first pattern characterises a way of speaking often found in Germany: long, strong, and rich in detail. When one person speaks, others listen silently, before someone else starts on another long turn.

The second pattern is said to be more common in Sweden: less dominated by single speakers, shorter and sharper than the German pattern, but with listeners similarly silent. The longer silences between the turns may signal greater respect and caution in a more collectivist culture, and an unwillingness to stand out as a stronger individual than the rest.

The final pattern is said to be more common in France: longer, more expansive and more adversarial. In this pattern, speakers explore ideas and options from different perspectives and are more tolerant of interruptions from listeners.

Misunderstandings can clearly occur when these different types of communicator meet. Type 3s may find type 1s rather machine-like and uncreative. Type 1s and type 2s may see type 3s as rather disorganised, and rude in the way they interrupt and talk over others. Type 2s may be seen by both type 1s and type 3s as distant and difficult to engage.

Of course, these descriptions are stereotypes and such styles and clashes between styles cannot simply be reduced to national cultural differences. They can also happen as a result of differences in personal communication style, for example between a very talkative and unstructured extrovert on the one hand, and a very careful, concise and structured introvert on the other.

An international model: the interactive dialogue model

For dialogue to work effectively, there needs to be cooperation between the speaker and the listener. There are certain steps that speakers can take to include listeners. In the interactive dialogue model below, the speaker manages the length of speaking time carefully and introduces an active handover phrase. The aim is to create a process in which people can communicate openly and transparently.

THE INTERACTIVE DIALOGUE MODEL

Person 1 and Person 2 have a conversation. Person 1 starts talking and Person 2 listens. As a speaker, Person 1 does not talk for too long, and finishes talking with an active handover to Person 2 using a question, for example *What do you think?* The aim is to check understanding and involve the listener, creating interactive dialogue.

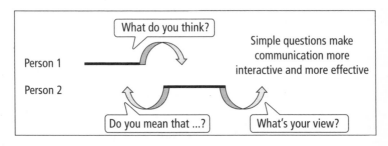

Person 2 does not disagree or give an opinion immediately and takes time to clarify or reformulate what has been said, by asking Person 1 a question, for example *Do you mean that … ?* This checks understanding and shows respect for Person 1's ideas. Then Person 2 can give an opinion. They avoid talking for too long and hand back actively after speaking with a short question, for example *What's your view?* And so the process continues.

Note

In this model both Person 1 and Person 2 listen actively, using phrases to show understanding *(I see)* and interest *(That's important because …)*. This builds a clearer and more positive dialogue.

4 STYLE

The final dimension that speakers have to consider is to what extent their personal speaking style is effective in their international contacts. People speak in different ways for both psychological reasons (for example, because they are more extrovert or more introvert) and because of cultural influences (for example, they have learned to be direct because their corporate culture is highly task-oriented).

Use the analysis below to profile yourself and reflect on your own communication style. It can encourage you to get feedback and to think more strategically about how you communicate internationally.

Your speaking style

Think about the way you speak in professional situations and work through these five steps. You will, of course, speak differently from one work situation to another, so try to think about how you speak *typically*.

1. Circle the word in each pair below that best describes your speaking style:

Physical		
	Fast	Slow
	Loud	Quiet
	Energetic	Calm
	Touching	Distant
	Smiling	Serious

Informational	Long and complex	Short and simple
	Analytical	Results-oriented
	Structured	Flexible
	Direct	Indirect
	Time-focused	Time-flexible
Psychological	Introvert	Extrovert
	Impersonal	Personal
	Open	Closed
	Emotional	Neutral
	Pushing	Helping

2. Ask an international colleague if he/she agrees with your self-evaluation.

3. Now that you have a picture of your style, note down how different international partners might interpret it (the positives and the negatives).

4. Think about how you may need to adapt your personal speaking style for your next meeting, presentation or negotiation in line with the results of point 3.

5. After your next meeting, negotiation, presentation, etc., get feedback from someone on your communication style. Were you clear? Did you have a positive or a negative impact? Then decide on an area that you need to improve.

Be aware that speaking fast presents significant problems for non-native speakers. The average native speaker uses around 250 words per minute in full flow. The average non-native speaker may be comfortable at around 100 words per minute. Slowing down is not patronising; it is essential if you want people to understand you.

It's not what you say, it's the way that you say it

The tone of your voice, your speech rhythm and your volume can significantly change the way in which people understand and interpret your words. Look at the ways in which these voice characteristics may be interpreted.

Volume   Some people think that loud speakers are arrogant.

Tone   Some people think that a hard tone is aggressive.

Pitch   Some people think that a lower pitch signals strength or maturity.

Fillers   Some people think that sounds like 'uh' or little laughs show insecurity.

Ask yourself:

- What impact does your voice have on your international business partners?
- What impressions and assumptions might it generate?
- Which of the above dimensions would it be useful for you to adapt to be a clearer communicator?

THE FINAL WORD

Successful international speakers think carefully about how they communicate. They consider the expectations, needs and English language abilities of the people who are listening to them – their communication customers.

They try to speak in a way which matches the specific profiles of different listeners or groups of listeners, making it easy to listen. Effective international communicators also need to be self-aware, to understand their own communication preferences and tendencies – to be long or short, to be simple or complex, to be loud or quiet – and have the flexibility to adapt. Finally, effective speakers seek feedback.

Most of us over-estimate our flexibility, our ability to modify our behaviours to the needs of others. One important way we can know if our communication style is confusing to international partners is to ask them: *Is my speed too high? Am I talking too much? Would you like me to repeat anything again*? And remember, if people ever show in later emails or actions that they did not understand, take that as a constructive criticism of your ability to speak clearly, not their lack of understanding.

3

LISTENING

*If we were supposed to talk more than listen,
we would have two tongues and one ear.*

Mark Twain, American author and humorist (1835–1910)

Listening is the foundation of effective communication. As children, we learn to listen before we can speak, read or write. But many professional people have rather poor listening skills. They sometimes find it difficult to concentrate on what the other person is saying. Perhaps they have little real interest in the other person's ideas. Often they are impatient to start talking themselves and give their own point of view. And, as native speakers, we are often too quick to talk rather than listen, particularly when our non-native speaker partners seem to need so much more time to formulate ideas. Whatever the reason, this lack of listening leads to misunderstanding, conflict and inefficiency in the workplace.

In this chapter we look at the nature and purpose of listening, and at how to become a more effective listener.

Before you read on, think about these questions:

1. Why should we listen to other people?
2. What kind of listener are you?
3. What stops us from listening effectively?
4. How can you become a better listener?

REASONS FOR LISTENING

Let us look at the benefits of listening effectively.

1 To get the information we need to complete a task

This is the most obvious reason for listening at work, and people generally do this quite well. It typically means listening silently, with occasional questions to check the accuracy of the information given, before going away to do a job. This is a kind of listening that generally benefits the listener more than the speaker, which is probably why it is easier to do.

2 To assess competence and trustworthiness

This is a key reason for listening in the business world. It involves analysing the expertise and the attitudes of speakers, and making judgements about them.

3 To show competence and trust

As listeners, we want to demonstrate our own expertise by showing that we understand complex issues. We also want to show our approach to business through positive agreement or constructive disagreement with what the speaker says.

4 To show respect and to build rapport

Taking time to listen to others is an act of respect, and shows your commitment to your relationship with the other person. However, listening styles differ. For example, speakers from more task-oriented cultures may expect listeners to show respect by being silent. On the other hand, people from more relationship-oriented cultures may expect listeners to be more active and to show a positive attitude, for example, by making comments like *That's interesting*. Using the wrong listening style can lead to confusion. Silent listening may be misinterpreted by a relationship-oriented speaker as a sign of hostility. Verbal feedback may be perceived as unnecessary 'noise' by a task-oriented listener.

5 To monitor the speaker's style in order to achieve better communication

The focus here is less on content than style. The objective is to analyse the speaker's verbal and non-verbal behaviour. Which words do they use? How fast do they speak? Is their message structured? How aware is the speaker of the listener? What kind of body language do they use? Listeners can then adapt their own styles to the speaker's, so that the speaker feels more comfortable and open communication is easier.

6 To understand how to influence others

Effective motivators and influencers try to understand other people's interests before speaking. For example, good salespeople often start by asking questions and listening carefully to the answers before trying to sell.

7 To empathise

Speakers sometimes just want a listener 'to be there for them', that is, to listen to the problem, to show understanding, and to share a difficult experience. In this role, the listener is primarily supportive of the other person, without having any personal advantage or interest.

8 To understand the mindset of the other person

This is about listening 'between the lines', that is, listening to what is *not* said, and analysing the attitudes, assumptions and values of the speaker. What do their words tell us about their attitudes to leadership, to teamwork, to business relationships, to risk, or to time? These things may not be said, but someone with a sensitive ear can learn a lot about them by listening.

9 To hear if our ideas are understood and valued

As listeners, we can also evaluate our own performance as speakers. When others misunderstand what we are saying, we need to deliver our ideas in another way. Of course, it may be that our ideas have indeed been understood but not accepted. So we also need to listen carefully for any clash of assumptions or values.

THE ROI (Return On Investment) ON LISTENING EFFECTIVELY IN THE WORKPLACE

Better relationships with more trust
More motivated staff
Higher productivity
Increased creativity
Improved quality
More efficient information flow
Fewer mistakes and lower costs
Happier customers

10 To give pleasure

Do people generally enjoy talking to you? Do others say that you are an easy person to talk to? Do people walk away from meetings with you with smiles on their faces? If people are motivated to talk to you, you are more likely to get the best from them. This means we need to reflect. Are we listening in a way which is motivating for the other person?

WHAT KIND OF LISTENER ARE YOU?

It is essential to be aware of your own listening style and of the impact that your style may have on others. Read these descriptions of three different kinds of listener below and decide which style is closest to yours.

People-focused listeners

This kind of listener focuses on supporting the speaker by being attentive to feelings and needs. He/She has a lot of patience and asks questions such as *What do you think?* or *How do you feel about this?* This helps speakers to give their views and to feel that they are being listened to. This person-oriented style may, however, seem unfocused to information-oriented and results-oriented speakers, who may not like too many 'vague' questions about feelings.

Information-oriented listeners

This kind of listener likes to collect and analyse information in order to understand the situation as fully as possible. They usually take the time to listen to all the information so that the right decision can be taken. This analytical approach may, however, overlook the emotional attitudes behind the information and seem cold or unsympathetic to some speakers.

Results-oriented listeners

The main interest for these listeners is to achieve their goals as quickly and efficiently as possible. They often have little patience for what they see as irrelevant information, and can be frustrated by speakers who talk for too long in an 'unfocused' way. Some speakers, especially those who expect listeners to show empathy or analytical skills, may see results-oriented listeners as pushy and arrogant.

Which type of listener are you primarily?

WHAT STOPS US FROM LISTENING EFFECTIVELY?

Read the Speaker–Listener dialogues below and think about why listening is not happening effectively in each case. Think in terms of the message, the speaker and the listener. Then read our analysis in the Answer key at the back of the book.

Dialogue 1
Speaker: *So, what do you think about my recommendation on pricing?*
Listener: *What? Oh, sorry. Look, I'm not sure I'm the right person to ask.*
Speaker: *But you're in charge of sales, aren't you?*
Listener: *Yes, but I'm really busy now. Can we discuss this tomorrow?*

Dialogue 2
Speaker: *So, the fifth aspect of this problem is ...*
Listener: *Sorry to interrupt, but what was the fourth aspect? I didn't catch that.*
Speaker: *The fourth aspect was finance. Remember?*
Listener: *Oh, that was number four. Sorry. Are there many more points?*

Dialogue 3
Speaker: *I think we need to look at the terrible problem that we have in our team.*
Listener: *I don't think we should use the word 'problem' here.*
Speaker: *OK, well let's say 'issue' then. We need to discuss how we can ...*
Listener: *Sorry, but this is a decision for the team leader, not for us. I suggest we arrange a meeting with her as soon as possible.*

BECOMING A BETTER LISTENER

The key to becoming a better listener is *attitude*. We need to believe that other people are really worth listening to, and that it is important to give others the chance to express themselves. We need to believe that it is useful to engage with others, and that both speaker and listener can learn and benefit from dialogue. Otherwise there is little chance of developing good listening skills.

Let us look at 11 principles of effective listening.

1 Empty your mind of your own thoughts when the other person begins to speak

Make yourself concentrate fully on what is being said. Focus on hearing interesting and important information. Try to discover the different levels of meaning in the message: move from the information on the surface to considering the feelings, attitudes and needs of the speaker. Respect what is said and see this as an opportunity to learn something new about the person.

2 Support the start of a conversation by encouraging others to talk

Do this by asking questions, as this creates golden opportunities for listening. You can tailor the kind of question you ask to your listening objective. For example, do you want to get information, assess the competence or mentality of the speaker, or build rapport?

3 Give others time to say what they want to say

Remember that it often takes longer to get ideas across in a foreign language: words have to be remembered, and sentences have to be formed. Try to become comfortable with the silence that others may need in order to formulate their ideas.

4 Respond to what is said

When we listen, we need to make two basic types of response. We need to show that we understand what has been said (*I understand*); and that we value what has been said (*I think this is important because* ...). Otherwise, speakers may become confused or unwilling to go on talking to us.

5 Give positive feedback, both verbal and non-verbal, in ways that the speaker will interpret as positive

Opinions about what makes positive feedback vary according to cultural norms and personality preferences. For example, what does silence mean? Does it indicate interested concentration or a lack of interest, or even hostility? Comments such as *Yes, that's interesting* or *Really?* may be intended and seen as a sign of positive politeness in some contexts, but as superficial and not genuine in others. Non-verbal behaviours, such as strong eye contact or smiling at the speaker, may also be viewed positively or negatively, depending on cultural context and personal preferences. Monitor the impact of your listening style and adapt it if it seems to be confusing or negative.

6 Clarify what is said

Never assume that you have understood something correctly. It is particularly important to clarify when working in a foreign language because speakers often do not use the words they really need. Also, when working internationally, it is sometimes difficult to understand the motivation of business partners, who may have very different values, attitudes and interests.

7 Use the 'keyword approach' to listening

Listen carefully to the words the speaker uses, and then use some of the same words to develop the conversation. This technique is not just about clarifying. If speakers hear their own words reflected back in a question or a comment, this can increase comfort and trust.

The following dialogue illustrates this technique. The words in bold are the key words that Natasha picks up from Karl's comments and uses to guide the conversation. This form of listening is a simple but powerful technique for keeping the listener concentrated and the speaker energised.

Karl: *OK, I'd like to focus on pricing in this meeting. We may need to reduce our prices a little next year.*

Natasha: *When you say* **'a little'***, Karl, how much do you mean? One or two of our main competitors radically undercut us in some markets.*

Karl: *You're right. I was thinking mainly of the French and the German markets, which are so important for us.*

Natasha: *OK, so shall we focus on the* **French and German markets** *for the moment? What do you suggest?*

Karl: *My feeling is that we need to look at a price cut of around ten per cent if we want to attract new customers who view us as too expensive at the moment.*

Natasha: *That's interesting. Of course, if we're talking about* **attracting new customers***, maybe we need to think about a different strategic approach.*

8 Develop conversations by asking questions and making relevant comments

Good listeners *create* opportunities for listening. Make sure that you engage others by asking questions that invite them to talk in depth about topics that *they* find interesting, not simply to deliver information that is interesting to you. Be careful, however, not to turn conversations into interviews by asking too many questions and putting pressure on the speaker.

9 Give yourself feedback on your own listening performance

Ask yourself the following questions as you listen. Am I fully concentrating on the other person or am I letting my mind wander away? Am I becoming impatient? Am I disagreeing too quickly with what is being said? Am I spending too much time preparing counter-arguments in my head? Am I asking the right questions and paying enough attention to the feelings behind the words? Self-coaching when listening is a good way to keep yourself engaged.

10 Know when to stop listening and end the conversation

Summarise as much as necessary to avoid any misunderstandings. Make sure that the conversation ends positively.

11 Control yourself

Keep your negative emotions under control, even if you feel the speaker is attacking you or not showing you respect. Try to remain calm and engaged by asking questions. Recognise that it may not be the speaker's intention to cause these feelings. Stop yourself saying *Yes, but … .* This could be a sign that you have stopped listening.

Try not to interrupt or otherwise disturb the speaker or communicate disrespect. Listen to yourself listening, and if you hear any of the unconstructive thoughts below, switch them off and re-engage with the speaker.

Rejection of relevance:	*This is boring.*
Contradiction:	*Yes, but …*
Changing the subject:	*That's enough about this. Let's talk about …*
Denial of feelings:	*You don't need to worry about that.*
Transfer to self:	*Let me tell you about something that happened to me.*
Advising:	*All you have to do is …*
Focus on time:	*I have other things to do.*

Energise yourself physically. If you feel tired or start to lose interest, move, change position, stand up and walk around if you can, breathe deeply a few times, or alter the mood of the moment by asking a provocative or fun question.

Take notes to maintain your concentration when listening to a long presentation or to a lot of speakers during a meeting. Structuring a speaker's ideas with some form of visual representation (bullet points, boxes, mind maps) is also a good way to improve your understanding and to remain engaged.

ARE YOU READY TO START LISTENING?

Effective listening needs commitment, effort and skill. The fact that so many professional people listen badly creates big risks – for leaders, teams, projects and profitability. So, how long does it take someone to become a better listener? Well, a karate instructor once said that he had to practise a new move 10,000 times before he had truly perfected it and it became an internalised competence that he could perform automatically. The message is clear. Becoming a good listener is a long journey for most of us. So why not make your next conversation your first step on your road to becoming a great listener?

4

COMMUNICATING NON-VERBALLY

The human body is the best picture of the human soul.

Ludwig Wittgenstein, Austrian-born philosopher (1889–1951)

The focus of this book is on the challenges of communicating internationally in English. However, a lot of communication is non-verbal. Indeed, non-verbal communication can sometimes be just as important as spoken communication – and it can be just as difficult to interpret, particularly across different cultures.

In this chapter we look at four of the main types of non-verbal communication and ask you to reflect on your own assumptions. You can build a 'personal non-verbal communication profile' to help you improve the clarity and effectiveness of your spoken messages.

Before you read on, think about these questions:

1. What different types of non-verbal communication are there?
2. How can we understand the body language of other people?
3. How can we use body language to support our own communication?

DRESS AND PHYSICAL APPEARANCE

People often make judgements about others based on physical characteristics such as skin colour, height, physique, hairstyle and clothing. In business, it is important to understand how others may interpret your appearance. You need to ensure that your 'look' is sending out the right messages about, for example, your authority and expertise. The impact of your message may be completely destroyed if your appearance is sending out the wrong signals to a particular group of people. At the same time, it is important not to make quick judgements about others simply because their appearances do not fit with your expectations.

Answer the following 'dress and appearance' questions and create part 1 of your personal non-verbal communication profile.

PERSONAL PROFILE – PART 1 Dress and appearance	Notes
In which ways does your 'look' communicate your individual personality and your cultural identity?	
What do you imagine that your international colleagues and contacts think about the way you look? (both positives and negatives)	
How could you change your appearance to have a better impact on international colleagues and contacts?	
What, for you, is a professional look? What is unprofessional?	
How do you react when others do not conform to your expectations? Are you happy with this? Could you improve on this?	

PLACE AND SPACE

Physical environment has a big impact on our communication and the way we see ourselves and others. Just think about what anyone's office space says about the occupant.

When working internationally, it is important to understand and respect the physical boundaries that individuals create for themselves and others. These boundaries can be defined in very different ways across cultures. In some organisations, private territories are marked by closed office doors with access rights controlled by personal assistants. In others, open doors and open plan offices may signal commitment (by the management if not the staff) to greater cooperation and teamwork.

There are also different views across cultures about how closely people can stand or sit next to each other, and about whether people may touch each other. Breaking such codes by, for example, sitting in the wrong chair, or standing in the wrong place, or patting the wrong person on the back, can communicate disrespect and weaken the impact of your verbal communication.

Now answer the following 'place and space' questions and create part 2 of your personal profile.

PERSONAL PROFILE – PART 2 Place and space	Notes
What cultural values does the physical environment in your organisation communicate?	
What does the organisation of your office tell visitors about you (and your colleagues)?	
How much space do you like to have between yourself and other people when you have a conversation?	
Which international partners might find your 'boundaries' uncomfortable?	
How could you adapt your place and space behaviours to have a better impact on international colleagues and contacts?	

BODY LANGUAGE

Body language has many dimensions. Take a look at the following list with examples. Which of the example behaviours do you see as positive and which negative? Why?

Gesture	pointing with a single finger, clenching a fist, giving a thumbs-up sign
Eye contact	maintaining gaze for a long period, looking down
Facial expressions	smiling, having one's mouth open when eating, closing one's eyes when listening
Posture	standing facing other people, sitting with one's feet on the desk, holding one's hand in front of one's mouth
Touch	shaking hands firmly, hugging, patting someone on the back, placing an arm round someone's shoulder
Movement	walking quickly, nodding when listening, shaking the head strongly from side to side to indicate you disagree
Energy and pace	talking quickly, walking slowly

Correctly interpreting the body language of other people is a big challenge. Specific gestures or facial expressions do not have clear meanings: crossed arms, for example, could be a sign of defensiveness or could simply show that someone feels cold. Cultural variations make things more complicated: smiling, for example, usually shows friendliness, but may sometimes be a sign of nervousness or a lack of seriousness.

Seeing the big picture

Do not try to interpret single gestures. Look at the whole range of signals that a person sends out through body language, tone of voice, movement and so on. If you think you see body language which is signalling a problem, check your understanding by asking questions such as *Sorry, is that OK?* or *What do you think?*

The second challenge is to make sure that other people receive a clear and positive message from the signals given by your body language. This is also difficult because people may interpret your behaviour based on their cultural codes or personal preferences, and so may interpret your intentions quite wrongly.

Synchronise verbal and non-verbal communication

Use gestures and facial expressions in the same way that you would use a visual on a flipchart or a PowerPoint slide – to make your message clear. If gesture is acceptable in the environment in which you are working, reinforce what you say with hand movements or facial expressions which are synchronised with key words in your message. For example, when you are giving lists of ideas or numbers – *first, second, third, ...* – use your fingers to count as you say the words in order to make your message clearer. Look at effective presenters on television or in business to get more ideas on how to connect the non-verbal and the verbal.

Communicate confidently

Speaking with a confident voice with clear projection, and stress on key words, is very important. Support this with confident gestures, posture and movements. Video yourself communicating in English and rate how confident you think you sound and look. Ask other people to give you feedback. Use your own self-feedback and others' thoughts to develop a list of areas to improve.

Signal respect clearly with flexible behaviour

You signal respect for another person by using non-verbal communication which others feel comfortable with. You can also make other people feel relaxed by mirroring their body language and adapting your style to theirs. This does not mean that you should imitate or mimic them. But by following their style, you can increase the chances of your communication being well-received.

Now answer these body language questions and create part 3 of your personal profile.

PERSONAL PROFILE – PART 3 Body language	Notes
Can you describe your own typical body language when you are in a meeting or giving a presentation, for example? Gesture: Eye contact: Facial expressions: Posture: Touch: Movement:	

Which features of your body language do you think
could confuse or irritate international colleagues and
contacts?

How could you adapt your body language to have a
better impact on international colleagues and contacts?

PARALANGUAGE

Wikipedia defines paralanguage as 'the non-verbal elements of
communication used to modify meaning and convey emotion'.
Paralanguage is about how the *way* you say something can change
the way that people interpret the words and sentences that you speak.
We mentioned some paralinguistic features in Chapter 3, for example, the fact that some people think that loud speakers are arrogant,
or that a hard tone is aggressive, or that sounds like 'uh' may show
insecurity. It is important to have a clear idea of your own paralanguage in order to understand how people may see you positively
or negatively. It is also important to think about whether you need to
adapt your behaviour in some way to make sure you create a positive
impression.

Now you can answer these paralanguage questions to create part 4
of your personal profile.

PERSONAL PROFILE – PART 4 Paralanguage	Notes
Describe your own typical way of speaking using the following key dimensions: Speed e.g. fast or slow Volume e.g. loud or quiet Tone e.g. soft or hard	
What impact – positive and/or negative – does your voice have on the people you work with?	
How could you adapt your paralanguage to have a better impact on international colleagues and contacts?	

FINAL THOUGHTS

We evaluate the non-verbal communication of other people consciously and unconsciously. We make judgements about their personalities and professional competence. And we often communicate these judgements through our own non-verbal communication without realising that we are doing so. For example, we may smile at someone we like or reduce the amount of eye contact we have with someone whom we do not like. Even if we do not say negative or positive things to another person, we may still communicate these feelings non-verbally.

This means that we need to manage both what we think and what our body does. We need to be aware of our feelings, particularly of our negative emotions, and to try to manage them as they happen. We also need to monitor what our body is doing. For example, if we are feeling bored in a meeting, we may start to lean back in our chair. If we realise this is happening, we can lean forward again and re-establish eye contact with other people. Being mindful in this way can help us to create a positive impact on our communication partners.

By observing other people closely when you are talking to them, you can check the extent to which they are engaging with you. But do not assume that you understand the meaning of what you see and hear. Ask questions to confirm how others are thinking and feeling, particularly if you think that someone is feeling uncomfortable or that there is a problem.

If you follow these steps, you will gradually improve your ability to understand the non-verbal signals that other people send out, and be more able to send out signals that support your own professional messages.

CASE STUDY 1

'DID YOU HEAR WHAT I SAID?'

CASE STUDY 1

Read this case study which illustrates some of the challenges which occur when communicating internationally. Then answer the questions and compare your answers with the case commentary.

◇◇◇

'Did you hear what I said?'

John Simons, head of HR, had just given a short presentation to a group of 35 international HR colleagues at a meeting in Zurich about his ideas for a new leadership competence model. He was well prepared – he had at his fingertips lots of funny anecdotes from colleagues about leadership failings in the company. And he had a new model to present which he had developed himself, based on the latest thinking from Harvard University research. Things seemed to start well:

Well, what I want to get the ball rolling with today is a question. It's probably not a question we put to ourselves that often but … bear with me for a few seconds, humour me. My question is, why do we actually bother to train leaders in our company? If leaders are born rather than crafted by training, maybe we're overlooking the obvious … recruitment, not development, is the real solution to our leadership deficiencies. Now, before my L&D colleagues decide to lynch me, let me explain a little bit where I'm coming from …

But not all's well that … starts well. During his introduction, John had made it quite clear that he wanted his audience to join in, to participate and comment on his ideas. That's why he said *Please interrupt me if you have any questions.* During the presentation he had said a few times *Any thoughts on this?* A few colleagues from the London and Chicago offices chipped in. But among the entire group of non-native English-speaking colleagues, not one question was asked during the whole presentation. Most people just sat staring at him with what seemed like a hostile stare.

At the close, one of his Dutch colleagues finally raised a hand to make a comment and ask a question:

I don't think this leadership model offers anything new. Why should we take it in Holland if it offers no extra value?

John struggled to bite his tongue. He had heard about the legendary Dutch resistance to any ideas coming from the headquarters before. He decided to make a stand:

The new model has the backing of the CEO. It's strategic and needs to be implemented by all of us.

Silence followed from the Dutch colleague. It seemed to John that he had taken the right decision in drawing a line in the sand. And with no more questions forthcoming from anyone, it was time to end the presentation.

Later John reflected on what to make of it all. Why so little feedback? Was he somehow too provocative at the start? Was his northern accent a problem? Did anyone outside the UK and US offices actually speak English? Was he just too boring? Was he a little on the rude side to the Dutch HR director? John headed for the evening event rather despondently.

QUESTIONS

1. What do you think of John's general reaction to his presentation experience?

2. How well do you think John handled the question from his Dutch colleague?

3. How well do you think he understood the behaviour of the rest of his audience?

4. How effective do you think John's use of English was when communicating to the non-native English speakers in the audience?

5. John wanted his audience to interact and give feedback on his ideas. How might be have handled his presentation differently to achieve this?

OVER TO YOU

Non-native speakers constantly complain that it is difficult for them to understand the English of their native speaker colleagues.

1. How can you find out how difficult your English is for your non-native speaker colleagues to follow?

2. What is the most important thing that you can do to make your English easier to understand?

COMMENTARY

1. John reacted quite typically to such a challenging moment of inter-national communication – with a slight sense of failure and sadness. It is excellent that he took time to reflect and think through possible causes of the problem. Interestingly, he avoided the easy solution of simply 'blaming' his audience, even recognising that he might have been mainly responsible (his northern accent was difficult to under-stand, he was 'too boring'). Taking time to reflect creatively and avoid-ing an over-fast negative judgement of the other party is essential for international communicators. However, John should have remained positive and headed for the evening event with more focus. When things seem to go wrong, it is important to avoid being negative and stay curious, to go to people and check why things happened as they did, to ask for feedback, to learn.

2. We do not have enough information to fully assess how effectively John handled the question from the Dutch colleague. But the man-ner that he chose carries risks.

The first risk is that John relied on reported and rather negative information about the individual to inform his decision on how to respond. Do not prejudge others. Build up a balanced picture based on your own experience of the person.

Secondly, John answered the question without really under-standing the intention and context of the speaker. At first sight, the question seems challenging but the perceived directness may be typical for the Dutch individual and his/her culture. There is often a positive intention behind directness, for example to contribute openly and honestly in order to reach a good result. The speaker may also have a point. Perhaps the model in Holland was better than the new model. It was an opportunity for John to learn something and enrich his new model still further. The fact is, John does not know. He took no time to clarify the purpose of the question and to engage in dialogue with the questioner. As a result, he left the presentation not understanding the real reason for the question nor how the Dutch colleague feels about his answer.

3. All of John's explanations are plausible. There are two interesting points to note. His first reactions were to interpret the situation negatively. It is important to realise that when behaviours from people from other cultures do not correspond to our own – they are silent when we are loud, they are serious when we smile, and so on – it may actually derive from a positive motivation, in this case, for example, it could be simply respect for authority.

Secondly, John did not consider his language to be an issue. So often native speakers overlook the language problem. They think they speak slowly, they think they speak simply. The simple truth is that they remain far too complex for the average non-native speaker.

4. We only have a small part of John's actual presentation but we can quickly identify a number of problems with his use of English for non-native speakers, even in such a short segment.

Overuse of idiomatic expression

Idiomatic expression is more difficult for non-native speakers than more standard literal expressions. Rather than *get the ball rolling,* it would be clearer to use *start.* Rather than saying *Let me explain a bit where I'm coming from*, it would be better to say *Let me explain what I mean.*

Complex sentence structures

John not only uses idiomatic expressions, but he embeds them in rather complex structures. Take a look at the following examples:

What I want to get the ball rolling with today is …
Better: *I would like to start with …*

Bear with me for a few seconds
Better: *I will explain in a moment*

In addition, John's use of rhetorical question structures (*Why do we bother*), with embellished logic (*If leaders are …*) creates unnecessary complexity for an audience having to decode this in a foreign language. It is better to be simpler, more direct and less … clever.
Better: *The topic of my presentation today is the new competence model I have developed following recent Harvard research. There are three main parts to the presentation … .*

Use of vocabulary likely to be unfamiliar

Non-native speakers learn common and more standard expressions when they learn English. Unfortunately, native speakers have a very broad vocabulary and happily integrate less common words, making their message very difficult to understand. Take a look at the following examples:

bother to
Better: *make an effort to*

overlooking the obvious
Better: *We are not seeing what is very clear*

leadership deficiencies
Better: *leadership problems*

5. The first thing that John should have done is to adapt his expectations about audience interaction during professional presentations. Rather than push audiences to confirm to his needs, he might have started by thinking about what might make *them* comfortable.

As already indicated, non-interaction is the norm in some cultures. For non-native speakers, speaking aloud as a member of an international audience is stressful and intimidating, and many will simply remain silent. If John had decided that he needed interaction, he could have networked with important individuals before the event in order to encourage participation. He could also have decided to get feedback after the event rather than during it. If he had wanted some interaction during the presentation, then integrating an exercise or activity such as break-out sessions or 'talk to a partner', then asking directly for feedback on these conversations, would have been more likely to produce the process John was originally looking for.

5

BUILDING RELATIONSHIPS

'If you can be interested in people, you can own the world.
Jay Abraham, US marketing expert

Relationship-building skills across cultures can be as important for professional success as technical skills. It is vital for us to think carefully about how we build and develop positive, lasting relationships with the people whom we work with – colleagues, managers, suppliers, customers and others.

In this chapter we focus on how to manage the first face-to-face meeting with a new contact, the opening moments of a business relationship. In following chapters in this section we look at other dimensions to professional relationships, including networking and building trust.

Before you read on, think about these questions:

1. How do you build professional relationships? What is your style?
2. What are the phases of developing a conversation with a new business contact?
3. Are there any differences in the way that men and women build professional relationships?
4. What specific skills do you need to build relationships across cultures?

RELATIONSHIP-BUILDING STYLES

People at work have very different views of what professional relationships are for. As a result, they approach first meetings with very different ideas about the kind of relationship they want to develop. Some want to become friends quickly. Others view their private lives as completely separate from the office and work relationships. These different preferences are influenced by both personality and cultural factors.

On the one hand, people who are very focused on results may well place less emphasis on relationships. On the other hand, people who place a lot of emphasis on relationships may need to remind themselves, or to be reminded, of the main reason for working – to get results.

People from more collectivist cultures may emphasise group ties more than those from more individualist cultures. Different attitudes to hierarchy will also have an impact. Senior people in more authoritarian cultures may expect formal deference to be shown to them in first meetings, while more senior people in more egalitarian cultures may well prefer a much more informal approach.

THE FOUR PRIMARY MOTIVATIONS FOR RELATIONSHIP BUILDING

Elias Porter, creator of relationship awareness theory, was an expert in the psychology of interpersonal relationships. He says that people are driven by very different motivations to form and develop relationships. Understanding these different motivations can help us to manage first meetings more effectively.

Try to identify your own main relationship motivation and communication style from the four descriptions below. While you are reading, think about what international colleagues and customers may like or dislike about your relationship-building style.

Motivation type 1: Supportive-Caring

For these people, the main motivation when building relationships is to support and help others. They feel good when they see others feeling good. In first meetings with visitors to the office, for example, they may make a lot of effort to check that other people are happy. They offer coffee, check if accommodation arrangements are alright, are keen to offer extra help, and so on. They may ask a lot of polite questions to make others feel welcome and accepted. They like to talk about what other people want to talk about.

> **WARNING!**
> These people may appear to some others as superficial and too friendly, perhaps even as nervous or lacking in confidence. But remember that they communicate with a positive intention – to be polite and to make others happy.

Motivation type 2: Assertive-Directing

For these people, the main motivation in building relationships is to get things done, to get results by influencing other people, to organise, and to make an impact. They see themselves as capable and in charge, ambitious and persuasive. In first meetings they are happy to talk and be heard. They can be very motivated when there is an exchange of opinions on a topic that they feel they know something about. They are happy to listen to others who share their view of the world but can also quickly become bored, especially with those who go into too much detail or who offer an alternative point of view. They are often quite sure that their way is right and can be difficult to persuade otherwise.

> **WARNING!**
> These people may seem to some others to be rather arrogant, pushy and self-centred, particularly in more indirect cultures. But they are very driven and have the vision and the capability to achieve a lot.

Motivation type 3: Analytical-Autonomous

For these people, the main motivation in building relationships is to protect their own freedom and sense of independence. They usually feel better when things are structured and under control. Their communication style in first meetings may be reserved. Keeping quiet is their way of maintaining a sense of autonomy and of showing respect for the independence of others. In discussions they may take more time to think about things than others and may prefer to focus on more familiar and practical topics rather than discussing subjects that they know little about. They may be good at discussing and analysing details, but less engaged when it comes to more creative brainstorming.

> **WARNING!**
> These people may come across to some others as too quiet, or even defensive, uninterested and critical of others, particularly in cultures where individuals are expected to be 'louder' and to confidently self-market their own abilities. Yet one of their main aims is to allow other people space, out of their respect for their independence.

Motivation type 4: Flexible-Connecting

For these people, the main motivation in building relationships is learning, and they are ready to be very flexible in order to learn from and about others. They see themselves as curious, open to change and ready to compromise in relationships. They are happy to adapt their behaviour to manage complex situations. In first meetings they try to 'fit in' and to adapt to whatever others wish to talk about and do. They will show interest in other people's points of view to demonstrate this. They often have a group focus and will work to create harmony between group members.

> **WARNING!**
> These people may seem to some others as difficult to judge, lacking direction, possibly very political, and too changeable. But they are also very open, sometimes highly creative, and very helpful in creating a positive group dynamic.

MANAGING FIRST CONTACTS

There are many different types of first meeting, from an unplanned greeting in an office corridor to an organised event such as a project kick-off meeting. Here we look at how to manage six different phases of a first meeting, remembering that we have to adapt our approach to each specific individual, business and cultural context.

Many people now work as part of a virtual team with team members spread across the globe (see Chapter 17). There are fewer opportunities to get to know people and their work situations, and misunderstandings can easily arise. In such situations, it is essential to get as much advantage as possible from face-to-face meetings, in order to build mutual understanding and respect.

PHASE 1: PREPARING THE GROUND

There are three stages in good preparation.

1 Research

Find out about the person you are going to meet. Use the internet or intranet, and talk to colleagues or other contacts to get background information on the person's outlook, experience, competence and current priorities.

2 Pre-meeting contact

You might send an email before you meet a new contact to 'break the ice' and to create a positive atmosphere for your face-to-face meeting. Keep the email short and simple, especially if you are unsure of the individual's English language skills.

3 Focus

Prepare to focus completely on the person when you meet them, giving them your full attention. Things will start well if you show interest in and respect for the person right from the start. First impressions count.

PHASE 2: INTRODUCING YOURSELF

Personal introductions generally involve a spoken element (giving your name and/or origin: *I'm Peter Brown from the London office*) and a non-verbal component, for example, bowing or shaking hands.

Before you introduce yourself, decide which name or names to use, for example your first and/or your family name. Always say your name slowly and clearly so others can hear how it is pronounced. It can be very helpful to give your business card at the same time so that your counterpart can read your name. If your name is long, or could be difficult to pronounce, it will help if you offer a simpler form: *Please call me …* Your contact may also wish to hear an academic or job title such as Doctor or Head of Finance.

When working internationally, find out about protocols of role and hierarchy: who starts the introductions, and who introduces people to each other. The most senior person may have to handle the introductions. Also find out whether there should be an exchange of gifts.

First meetings can be a particular challenge for non-native speakers who do not feel so confident about their English. If you do feel more comfortable, you can be proactive and introduce contacts to each other, for example *Oleg, have you met Touria?*

PHASE 3: STARTING SMALL TALK AND DEVELOPING THE CONVERSATION

A host can start a conversation by asking about travel and offering refreshments before moving into the next phase of talking about different personal and professional topics. You can develop a conversation in many different ways, depending on the person in front of you. But you need to find the right topic. One way to do this is to:

1. look for a subject to talk about, focusing firstly on safe topics like travel to the venue, work, the weather, etc.

2. develop the topic with follow-up questions

3. find things you have in common in order to create mutual understanding.

To find the right safe topic, ask some exploratory questions to see what people like to talk about. Some people like to talk about their last holiday. Others want to keep strictly to business topics. Focus on a topic that the other person seems to respond well to. And be sensitive to the pace of the conversation. Some people are much more comfortable with silence than others.

Remember also that people think and talk about the same topic in different ways. For example, some people like to talk about their interest in the local culture. Others will see it as an opportunity to talk about the time spent with their family. Some will just complain about prices. Whatever people are interested in, try to share similar experiences or opinions.

Your aim here is to establish rapport, which Wikipedia defines as 'a commonality of perspective or being on the same wavelength as the person you are talking to'. Rapport involves people establishing a positive relationship and mutual understanding, leading to similar behaviour and shared thinking. Indeed, psychological research shows that people sharing rapport may move in the same way, share a common body language, and communicate with the same physical 'rhythm'.

LUNCH FOR TWO: SMALL TALK STRATEGIES TO GET THE CONVERSATION GOING

Look at the following conversation between two colleagues having lunch during an international project meeting. How many small talk strategies can you identify in this conversation? Compare your answers with those in the Answer key at the back of the book.

Jean: *So, Sam, how's the project going?*

Sam: *Fine, thanks, Jean. Everything's on schedule at the moment.*

Jean: *Excellent. No problems with the software installation?*

Sam: *We had a few questions at the start but nothing serious. How about your work?*

Jean: *We've finished.*

Sam: *Finished? Great. You must be pleased.*

Jean: *Absolutely. It was a tough project.*

Sam: *Yes, I can imagine. Still, we'll have to find you something else to keep you busy, Jean!*

Jean: *Yes, thanks very much for that thought. Shall we order?*

PHASE 4: GETTING DOWN TO BUSINESS

The length of the small talk phase varies according to the preferences of the people involved. In some cultural contexts, it may be important to invest hours, days or even weeks in the process of getting to know each other. In more task-oriented environments, it may only take a few minutes before people get down to business. Whatever the context, it is critical that the bridge from small talk to business takes place in a way that everyone feels comfortable with. A standard way to manage this is to say *Shall we get down to business now?*

PHASE 5: SAYING GOODBYE

Once your business has been concluded, it is time to say goodbye. Some people indicate this moment by using words such as *Right* or *OK*, followed by a pause. They may also signal this physically by, for example, putting all their papers away or starting to look at their mobile phone.

But cultural, linguistic and personality factors may make it quite difficult to know when someone wants to end a conversation. Hesitation and silence could simply indicate that your contact is trying to remember a word. Asking questions such as *What are your plans for the rest of the day? Are you going back to the hotel?* or *Shall I call a taxi for you?* can help to find out whether the other person wants the conversation to end.

As the conversation finishes, it may be important to use an explicit and positive statement such as *It was good to see you* or *I think that was a useful meeting.* You can also refer to a future event by saying *See you next month* or *I'll call you next week.*

PHASE 6: FOLLOW UP

Relationships are not made in first meetings. They take time and commitment to develop in follow-up meetings and by email (see Chapters 13 and 14). Choosing which individuals to build stronger relationships with is part of networking and is examined in the next chapter. How to move to a deeper level of trust is examined in Chapter 5.

RELATIONSHIPS AND GENDER

American linguistics professor Deborah Tannen writes about the communication styles of men and women. She believes that men and women manage relationships and social conversation in quite different ways. Although there are great dangers in over-generalising, and although the context in which she is working is North American, it is interesting to reflect on what Tannen has to say, and on how far our own behaviour and the behaviour of people we know conforms to these stereotypes.

Tannen argues that, for women, conversations are about establishing connections and negotiating relationships. Women express friendship by telling each other what they are feeling and what happened during the day. The emphasis is on finding similarities and matching experiences.

On the other hand, Tannen argues that, for men, talking is primarily a way to maintain independence and to negotiate and maintain status within the social order. The focus for men, who often compete to hold centre stage, is on demonstrating knowledge and skills, or simply on giving important information.

Because the two world views which she describes are so far apart, both sides can feel frustration when dealing with the other. These are some of the areas of possible misunderstanding.

1 Asking for help

Women may be more likely to ask questions when they need help. Men may view asking questions as showing a lack of knowledge and competence, and as a sign of weakness.

2 Offering support

Tannen suggests that men may feel worried by offers of support. They may interpret such offers as a suggestion that they are not competent to do a job independently. Women, on the other hand, may view offers of support more as gestures of solidarity and intimacy.

3 Discussing problems

Women discuss problems not necessarily to find solutions but to share feelings and to be listened to. When men hear about problems, they are quick to offer solutions and may not understand why women react negatively to advice.

4 Building arguments

According to other research findings, many women support their opinions during discussions with examples or cases from their personal experience. Their male colleagues often see these arguments as too subjective.

TEST YOUR RELATIONSHIP-BUILDING SKILLS
The Centre for Intercultural Learning at the Canadian Foreign Service Institute defines a number of relationship-building skills for those working across cultures. Look at the checklist on page 73 based on the Centre's research and decide how far you use these relationship skills in your own international working. Score yourself from 1 (low) to 7 (high).

RESULTS OR RELATIONSHIPS?

Professionals who wish to be successful at work need to focus both on results and relationships. How far do you think you get the balance right?

An interculturally effective person ...	Score 1–7
1 has a relationship-building strategy	
- makes an effort to socialise with individuals from other cultures (will arrange meetings with individuals and find time to meet the wider communities in other cultures at every opportunity)	_____
- does not spend too much time abroad with fellow expatriates	_____
- does not become isolated from other cultures	_____
2 has a language strategy	
- invests time in learning the local language when abroad and can manage simple phrases and some basic conversation	_____
- will regularly ask for translations or the meanings of words in the local language	_____
3 knows other cultures	
- is able to describe key social protocols and codes of other cultures which are different from the home culture	_____
- is able to assess the importance of relationships and style of relationship building in other cultures	_____
4 is sensitive to stereotypes	
- understands how people from their home culture may be viewed in other cultures	_____
- is able to avoid stereotypical thinking about people from other cultures which could lead to negative judgements	_____
5 knows how he/she is seen in other cultures	
- will ask for feedback on his/her behaviour to check that it is appropriate for other cultures	_____
- will get positive feedback from international colleagues that he/she is friendly and fits well into other cultures	_____

Developing your skills

If your score is lower than 5 in any of the above dimensions (or less than 50 overall), you should think about how you can build upon your strengths and also how you can improve in the areas where you are not so strong.

6

NETWORKING

We are caught in an inescapable network of mutuality, tied in a single ... destiny. Whatever affects one directly, affects all indirectly.

Martin Luther King, American Baptist minister
and civil rights leader (1929–68)

Many people think their networking skills are not good enough. This is strange because most people understand that developing an international network of relationships is a key success factor in business.

So, what stops people from networking? Some individuals for personality reasons feel uncomfortable approaching strangers. In some business cultures it may be usual to maintain a professional distance from others. Others simply say they do not have enough time for networking, which often means that they do not *make* enough time for it.

Additionally, many people do not fully understand the processes of networking. If people do not know how to network, then they will not do it enough.

In this chapter we present some guidelines for a very proactive style of networking across cultures, and look at how such an approach can help to develop your performance and that of others to deliver measurable business results.

Before you read on, think about these questions:

1. What are the main benefits of networking?

2. Which people do you include in your international network?

3. What conversational skills do good networkers have?

4. How can you make your networking deliver results?

THE FOUR Ps OF PROACTIVE NETWORKING

There are four key principles to think about when you are building a network.

1 PURPOSE

The purpose of networking is to deliver tangible business benefits, for you or for your organisation. Networking is about developing the right kinds of relationship with the right kinds of people. It can enable information to flow more efficiently inside an organisation. But remember that it should be handled with integrity, and it should support the ethical principles of your organisation.

Because the purpose of networking is to get better business results, you should think carefully about your aims. Do you want to create a network that generates sales? Do you want to create job opportunities for yourself? Do you want to increase your influence within your organisation in order to promote and support your projects?

Defining a clear purpose will help you to give focus to your networking activities. This does not mean that you will necessarily see the results of your networking quickly or easily. But it is still a networking principle to have clear objectives and to regularly track your progress towards these objectives.

2 PEOPLE

There are two main approaches to networking, which we can call 'hunting' and 'fishing'.

'Hunting' people is a targeted approach and involves defining carefully who we want to connect with, identifying where they can be found, and finding ways to get introduced, for example by getting an invitation to a special event, offering to speak at one, and so on.

'Hunting' has clear benefits but also risks. We should in principle focus on key people and create a core network. But organisations are complex, and key decision-makers are not always easy to identify. Changes in company strategy can also suddenly bring us into contact with new parts of the organisation.

So it can be advantageous to go 'fishing' instead. This involves casting our net as widely as possible, and helping opportunities to arise more than creating them directly. It means making contact with people even when there is no obvious immediate benefit, for example, by talking to visitors passing through your office or spontaneously joining a group for lunch.

There may be tangible gains to this approach: unforeseen business opportunities may come your way. But there are also intangible advantages: this kind of 'seeding' can build your reputation as someone who is competent, experienced and nice to be with. This is something you can use when a specific need arises.

3 PERSPECTIVE

People often do not invest enough time in networking because they have the wrong perspective. Successful networkers recognise that the people side of business is important, that you cannot succeed alone, and that you need others to give you information and support. Once you see this, you will start to give the necessary time and energy to building your network.

But giving time is not enough. A lot of people think about their networks in the wrong way. If you only think about what you can get from other people, they will soon start to feel that they are being used and will drop away, possibly damaging your reputation as they go. Networking should be seen as a way of delivering *mutual* benefits. This has a big impact on how you communicate with the people in your network.

4 PATIENCE

Relationships do not develop overnight. Networking is much more than a quick handshake at a social event. It demands effort over the medium and long term. Relationships have to be looked after and encouraged to grow. Successful networkers have the patience to wait for results.

USING CONVERSATION TO NETWORK

Networking is about having lots of good conversations with lots of people. So the first challenge is to create opportunities for such conversations to take place. Both direct and indirect approaches are possible.

A direct approach could be to set up a lunch or dinner meeting by asking a contact you have identified. An indirect approach may involve making requests such as *Would it be possible to meet your head of sales?*

Different people choose different approaches. If you feel comfortable about marketing yourself, you may prefer the direct approach. On the other hand, the cultural context may not always permit this. An indirect approach may work better if an intermediary can really help you to set up a meeting with the person you want to talk to.

Unplanned opportunities for conversation arise every day: in the company restaurant or canteen (where you decide to sit affects who you meet); at large meetings (which group you join for a coffee affects who you talk to); or in the corridors as you pass groups of colleagues talking. In all these situations, it helps to be a good reader of group dynamics. Remember that such encounters are challenging when trying to build networks with people in other countries. In this context, a more planned approach may be necessary.

1 CONVERSATION AND GROUP DYNAMICS

When good networkers enter a room, they can quickly assess who is available for conversation and who is in a closed dialogue which should not be interrupted. *Networking Like a Pro: Turning Connections Into Contacts*, by Misner, Alexander and Hilliard, contains useful guidance on how to deal with this kind of situation.

You have just entered a room full of strangers having coffee before the start of a business seminar. (You are on the right in the diagram here.) Which of the groups of people (A–E) can you approach and engage in conversation? Go to the Answer key at the back of the book for an answer.

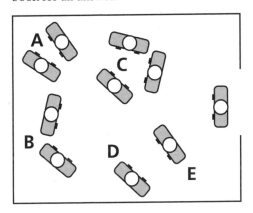

2 BREAKING THE ICE

Once you have identified an individual or a group to talk to, you need to be able to approach and engage the other person or people in conversation.

What you say to break the ice depends, first of all, on whether you are introducing yourself to new contacts or meeting people who know you. There are no golden rules, only a number of options to consider, depending on your sense of the particular person and of the context. Take a look at the two approaches in this table. Which of these would you be happy to use?

The 'hard' approach	
Connect quickly and explicitly to the other person's network. Show knowledge of the person. Highlight the reason for the conversation.	*Hello, I'm Lorenza Brunello. I've worked with a colleague of yours, Peter Pilger, and he said it would be good for us to meet as we're both running projects in China.*

The 'soft' approach	*Enjoying the conference? I've just*
Focus on the immediate context.	*been to a session on projects in*
Stay 'off topic'.	*China. I found it really fascinating*
Identify common interests.	*since I'm having a few problems*
	there with my own project.

3 MANAGING CONVERSATIONS

Effective networkers need to do the basics well: speaking clearly and listening effectively (see Chapters 2 and 3). However, there are added dimensions to speaking and listening for networking purposes.

Speaking

Good international networkers need to do three things when speaking.

1. **To be interesting.** Good networkers are memorable and engaging. They have interesting stories and anecdotes with useful facts and figures. They show self-confidence. They want the listener to remember what they say and to want more. Take care to consider how to handle more hierarchical contexts. For example, it may be more important to show interest in another than actually 'be' interesting yourself in some social gatherings.

2. **To offer value.** Good networkers provide information, insights and possible contacts that are useful in some way to the listener: *Would you like me to send you a copy of that report?* Networkers make themselves useful for other people to know: *I could help you with that if you want.*

3. **To build rapport.** Good networkers focus on things that the speaker and listener have in .common. They communicate facts and feelings as a way of building openness and trust.

How good are your speaking skills for networking? Think about your answers to these questions:

- Which of my life experiences will engage others? Why is this so?
- What are my views on doing business successfully? What can others learn from me?
- What have I learned from others in my network that I can pass on?

Listening

Effective listening for networking is based on concentrating, and on asking questions to identify business opportunities. As you ask your questions, take mental notes about the person's background, motivation and needs. Then think about ways in which you might be useful to them and ways in which they might be useful to you. Look at the topic areas in the table below and think of some questions you could ask for each one.

Listening for different topics

Topic	What you are listening for
Job and company	Identify overlaps of responsibility and challenge between you and them which could signify mutual interest. What is their status in the organisational and social hierarchy?
Professional experience	Important to get the bigger picture of the person – what are their values and attitudes?
Existing networks	Who do they know? How influential are they?
Approach to networking	Are they politically intelligent? Does networking turn them off?

4 CLOSING AND FOLLOWING UP

Effective networkers are good at finishing conversations on a positive note: *It was really good to meet you and to discuss the project.* Good networkers also focus on next steps: *I'll send you that information.* But if you promise to do something for the other person, then do make sure that you do it! Empty promises will damage your reputation.

After each networking conversation, you need to decide whether to keep the contact in your network. If so, keep a summary of who they are, how they can be useful to you, and how you can help them. Write down key professional and personal facts about the person as soon as you get an opportunity, for example on the back of their business card, and then convert this into a longer summary, which you can keep in a database. An example of such networking notes is given on page 82. How do your networking notes compare to these?

> Peter (call him Pete) is director of HR at Swedish Telia. Late 40s. Responsible for talent management. Strong international experience: worked in China for two years. Interested in support to develop an international leadership concept but not a great fan of intercultural training. Lives in centre of Stockholm Loves football: contact him next time Sweden plays. Action: Send a short summary of ideas and call him by end of June. He's open to a visit in autumn.

If people are worth contacting, then send an email within a week of the first meeting. If you use social networking sites (such as Linkedin or Xing), invite people to add you to their network. When you contact them, make sure that you include a reference to when you met, mention something positive about the meeting, and offer a clear benefit to the recipient and a proposal for future contact. Look at the sample email on page 83, which uses a plain and simple internationally-friendly English.

NETWORKING – A TWO-WAY PROCESS

Networking is a process that takes time, planning, a lot of patience, and a degree of faith. You will often not see immediate results. To get things moving, you have to be proactive and offer support to others, encouraging them to then support you. You can offer support, for example, by volunteering to help with tasks, putting people in touch with an expert who can help solve a problem they have, emailing them a useful article, recommending an interesting conference, or even finding a project you can work on together.

How many times have you done any of these things with your network contacts in the last month? If you cannot remember, then you have just identified your first task for the next few days. Good luck!

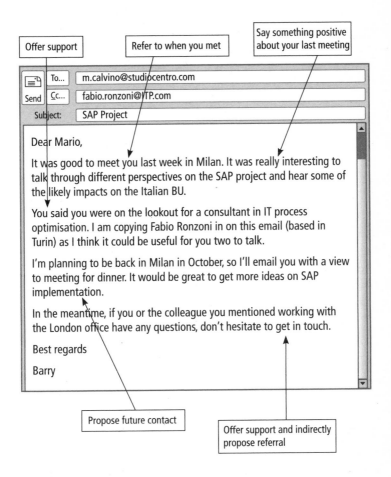

Offer support

Refer to when you met

Say something positive about your last meeting

To... m.calvino@studiocentro.com

Cc... fabio.ronzoni@ITP.com

Subject: SAP Project

Dear Mario,

It was good to meet you last week in Milan. It was really interesting to talk through different perspectives on the SAP project and hear some of the likely impacts on the Italian BU.

You said you were on the lookout for a consultant in IT process optimisation. I am copying Fabio Ronzoni in on this email (based in Turin) as I think it could be useful for you two to talk.

I'm planning to be back in Milan in October, so I'll email you with a view to meeting for dinner. It would be great to get more ideas on SAP implementation.

In the meantime, if you or the colleague you mentioned working with the London office have any questions, don't hesitate to get in touch.

Best regards

Barry

Propose future contact

Offer support and indirectly propose referral

7

BUILDING TRUST

*You must trust and believe in people,
or life becomes impossible.*

Anton Chekhov, Russian short story writer,
playwright and physician (1860–1904)

If you ask business people for the essential ingredient that enables international teams and organisations to perform excellently, you will often get a one-word answer – 'trust'.

Without trust, expensive controls are needed to check on staff, information does not flow freely, and commitment can be reduced. With trust in place, people have the freedom to fulfil their roles, and to provide the cooperation and support to others to help them to reach their goals too.

In this chapter we look at some of the key dimensions of trust, using research by WorldWork, a consultancy in communication across cultures. We also examine how you can increase trust in your team and organisation.

Before reading on, think about these questions:

1. What is trust?
2. What makes people trust each other?
3. Which communication strategies can help to develop trust when working internationally?
4. What can make it difficult to develop trust in organisations?

WHAT IS TRUST?

This question is not easy to answer. First, we need to remember that trust is not optional. It is mandatory, and for one simple reason: because we cannot do everything ourselves. I trust others to fly the planes and drive the trains I travel in. I trust my IT department to configure my desktop PC correctly. We have to trust other people.

Fundamentally, trust involves interdependence. It means being confident that other people will meet our positive expectations: to drive carefully, to keep information confidential, to deliver a work report on time, and so on. The downside is that we put ourselves at risk, since someone could betray our trust. The upside is that we can take decisions: to get on the plane, and to plan our working week based on the assumption that the report will be delivered on time. Trust allows us to organise our lives and to get things done.

There are different kinds of trust, which operate at both emotional and intellectual levels. The relationship-based trust we place in family members or partners is very different from the professional trust we may place in colleagues, or the more impersonal trust we may place in institutions such as airlines, banks, governments and religious bodies.

Trust is also situational. We may trust a particular person in one situation but not in another. I might trust you to stand in for me in a meeting, but I might not trust you to drive my new car.

BUILDING TRUST AT WORK

What does all this mean for building trust at work? What factors make us have faith in some people but not in others? If we understand these factors, we may be able to speed up the process of building trust. Here we look at seven factors that can support the development of trust:

1 PEOPLE TRUST THOSE WHO ARE COMPETENT

This is so obvious that we may overlook it, but we are unlikely to trust others unless we believe they have the necessary skills.

Estimating someone's competence may sometimes be based on relatively superficial factors, for example, the wearing of a particular uniform – as in the case of pilots, doctors or the police – may be enough in some situations to create trust. At work, a title or job function may be enough. But for our faith in others to continue over time, we normally need proof that someone has the relevant competence and the judgement to use it properly. Trust in the workplace often has to be earned.

Tips for building competence-based trust

- At work, people need to understand and appreciate each other's skills and talents. Some international teams create an online 'team book', a database which can be accessed from anywhere which gives people useful information on team member competence and general background. Other teams hand round people's CVs or encourage members to discuss their professional experience and skills over dinner.
- Colleagues need to be given a chance to prove themselves and show that they can be trusted. For leaders, this means delegating responsibility. Also, as team members succeed, it is important to celebrate success so that competence is recognised and higher levels of trust can be developed.
- It is important to explicitly communicate your trust in other people's competence. Communicating about trust helps to create a trust culture.

2 PEOPLE TRUST THOSE WHO ARE SIMILAR TO THEM

We tend to instinctively trust what is known and similar, and distrust what is different. We are more likely to have faith in people who have the same background, approaches, values, interests and objectives as us. This is important to recognise when working across cultures. There can be unnecessary levels of suspicion when people with different values and working practices meet because it is easy to misinterpret others' behaviours. So it is vital to invest time in getting to know other people in order that we can understand and appreciate them more.

Tips for building similarity-based trust

- Create a working culture where people are encouraged to ask questions about each other's backgrounds, interests and experience in order to find similarities. They can then discuss how these may help to improve the team's performance.
- Deal with any distrust that may arise between individuals from different backgrounds. Encourage a positive attitude to diversity. If you hear negative judgements in your own office about colleagues in other international offices, challenge these and focus people back towards collaboration based on common experiences and goals.

3 PEOPLE TRUST THOSE WHO SHOW EMPATHY

We are more likely to trust people whom we believe have our best interests at heart. It is much more difficult to trust someone whom we think wants to hurt us in some way.

Tips for building empathy-based trust

- Take an interest in the lives of colleagues. See it as part of your responsibility to understand their professional and personal priorities and the pressures they are under.
- Show them that they are important to you. Communicate your readiness to help them.
- Be an advocate for others. Show understanding when people have problems managing their workload. As a leader, you may be able to take on more yourself, or to delegate to others to reduce the pressure on someone who needs support.

4 PEOPLE TRUST THOSE WITH INTEGRITY

We generally respect and trust those who are honest, who keep their promises, and whom we think act according to a just moral code. We trust team-oriented people who work for the group more than those who seem mainly interested in furthering their own careers.

Tips for building integrity-based trust

- Communicate clearly about ethics. If you are a leader, try to build a team culture explicitly around defined organisational values. Make clear when you can and when you cannot be open: some management information will be confidential and cannot be shared with team members. If you discuss openly the question of what you can and cannot tell other people, they will respect your judgement when you do feel the need to hold back information. This helps to build rather than damage trust.

- It is easy to say that you are going to be a fair, honest and team-oriented leader. But you must make sure that you really are all these things and that people recognise this.
- Give positive feedback and/or rewards.
- Encourage those who break the rules to respect the agreed values.

5 PEOPLE TRUST THOSE WHO ARE RELIABLE

Trusting others, or getting others to trust us, is difficult if people are unreliable. You are more likely to be entrusted with a task if you have always demonstrated your reliability with the same kind of task in the past. People will find you more difficult to trust if you are unpredictable.

Tip for building reliability-based trust

- This dimension of trust takes time to develop. You have to prove through your actions over time that you are reliable. This means that you keep your promises and act consistently. This is particularly important in the early phases of team interaction. In other words, practise what you preach.

6 PEOPLE TRUST THOSE WHO INVOLVE THEM

We are unlikely to trust someone whom we believe is not telling us the full story. We are also unlikely to trust someone who seems to be reluctant to share their true feelings.

Tip for building involvement-based trust

- Involvement means circulating and sharing key information openly and proactively, although be careful not to flood international colleagues with lots of unnecessary and complex emails. Remember, building trust is an emotional process as well as a rational and logical one. So it may be helpful to be open about your feelings as well as about the facts. Involving others in our feelings and showing an interest in theirs can help to develop greater trust.

7 PEOPLE TRUST THOSE WHO TRUST THEM

Trust creates trust. If we want people to trust us, it helps if they believe that we trust them. In other words, one of the best ways to develop trust in a team is to show trust in others, even before you really have enough information to do so. This can be risky, of course. People may let us down. But taking this kind of risk can speed up the process of building trust in a team.

Tips for showing trust

- Communicate often and openly the fact that you trust others, even if you are not 100 per cent confident of their ability.
- Be explicit about the fact that you want people to trust you.

THE INTERNATIONAL TRUST CHALLENGE

Creating trust can seem difficult in today's global business world. Working virtually, working across cultures, and being involved in complex change processes can all make the task of building trust more challenging than in the past.

Increasingly, employees are sceptical of the word 'trust', especially when the word is used by managers in organisations where there is a lot of internal politics, misinformation and a mentality of self-preservation.

But trust is essential. By thinking carefully about building trust, by talking explicitly about trust in your team or organisation – even formally developing a trust strategy – it is possible to achieve not only better relationships but also better performance.

8

MAKING DECISIONS

*Nothing is more difficult, and therefore more precious,
than to be able to decide.*

Napoleon Bonaparte, Emperor of the French (1769–1821)

In this chapter we look at how to make decisions in international meetings. Effective decision-making requires different competences. These include:

- organisational skills (planning meetings)
- facilitation skills (managing the meeting)
- management skills (tracking decisions to ensure that actions are implemented).

We also give you the opportunity to profile your decision-making style and think about how effective it is with your international partners. Before you read on, think about these questions:

1. Why is business decision-making becoming more difficult?
2. What facilitation techniques help to manage a discussion within a culturally diverse group?
3. What kind of decision-maker are you?
4. What is the best way to lead a decision-making meeting?
5. How can you ensure that decisions are taken and implemented?

DECISION-MAKING IS GETTING MORE COMPLEX

Business used to be simpler. The working environment was less complicated, and information could be collected and analysed more easily. Big decisions came top-down from senior management, and were carried out by middle managers and the rest of the organisation.

Nowadays, business is more international; the business environment is more complex and ambigious; decision-making is more challenging. This is why risk management is becoming more and more important. We often make decisions before we have all the information we need, and so these decisions have to be modified as we get more data.

The rise of the matrix organisation, with multiple reporting lines, means that a range of stakeholders can be involved in decision-making processes. The increasing cultural diversity of organisations also presents a challenge. Individuals from different departments and countries can enter a meeting with very different ideas about how it should be run and how decisions should be made.

MANAGING DIVERSITY IN DECISION-MAKING

Decision-making meetings can be run more effectively if the following questions have been answered and a clear and simple process has been agreed. There are different ways to get answers to these questions. It can be done collectively as part of the meeting itself, or handled in pre-meeting contacts between the leader and individual participants.

What is a decision?

In some cultures a decision is a binding commitment. In others it is simply a guideline and can be changed if the situation changes or if new information becomes available: for these people, the objective is to reach the best result, not to respect a past decision.

Who takes the decision?

For some people, decision-making is the responsibility of the leader. In more individualist cultures, people tend to think that individuals should take decisions in their areas of responsibility. Some people even feel that meetings reach better decisions if the leader is not present so that team members feel free to speak openly. In more collectivist cultures, people feel that the best decisions are reached when the whole group is involved. In more service-oriented cultures, customers may participate in decision-making because they are important stakeholders too.

How is a decision taken?

For some individuals, a structured decision-making process with a clear agenda and voting procedure is most effective. For others, it is better to be less systematic in order to be more creative. With some people, it is possible to speak very directly and yet still be polite, for example *That's completely wrong, Hussein.* For others, a less direct approach is seen as the polite way to respect feelings, for example *I understand what you're saying, Hussein. However, … .* Some people need to analyse risks in detail, in order to avoid making a mistake. For others, it is better to take decisions quickly and then correct any mistakes that have been made.

Where is the decision taken?

For some people, it is better to hold meetings at an organisation's head office, and combine this with other meetings. For others, it is better to rotate the location of key decision-making meetings around regional offices in order to develop understanding of the different working contexts of team members. Also, while some people are happy to take decisions in virtual meetings, such as audio or video conferences, others find it essential to meet face to face.

How are people informed of decisions?

For some individuals, it is enough to send the minutes of the meeting, or a short email with an attached presentation, to the relevant people, both participants and others. For others, it is better to inform those not at the meeting – team or department members and external customers and stakeholders – via a mix of face-to-face briefings and written communication.

There are no right or wrong answers here. What you do should depend on the outlooks and abilities of the people involved and the demands of the specific situation. People leading international meetings have to choose from the following **ABCDE** strategies to manage different expectations:

Adapt   Adapt your style to match the expectations of others.

Blend   Be flexible and mix different approaches together.

Co-create   Develop a new and unique meeting culture together.

Divide   Agree to do it 'my way' today and 'your way' next time.

Enforce   If necessary, use a 'pull' approach and tell people to do it 'my way'.

YOUR DECISION-MAKING STYLE

People take decisions in different ways across cultures. Rowe and Boulgarides in their book *Managerial Decision Making: A Guide to Successful Business Decisions* have tried to classify these styles. They stress the importance of values, needs and preferences in understanding why individuals take decisions in the way they do. Their model describes four main decision-making styles, based on whether an individual is more task- or more relationship-oriented, and on how complex he/she wants the information to be on which he/she bases decisions. The model below shows us different motivations behind decision-making.

Complex	ANALYTIC Strong need for achievement (needs challenges)	CONCEPTUAL Strong need for achievement (needs recognition)
Information	DIRECTIVE Strong need for power	BEHAVIOURAL Strong need for affiliation
Simple		
	Task oriented	*People oriented*

1 Directive

Directive decision-makers need power. They are usually very results-oriented but also need to feel that they are in control of others or can dominate them. They are not very tolerant of ambiguity and prefer to keep things pragmatic and simple. They tend to take decisions based on less information and fewer alternatives. They like to work fast and to feel that it is their decision and not someone else's.

2 Analytical

Analytic decision-makers need to achieve. Being challenged motivates them. They are more tolerant of ambiguity than the 'Directives' and are also more comfortable handling information. This means that they can tolerate higher information loads and a greater number of possible courses of action, which they will analyse in detail over a longer period.

3 Conceptual

Conceptual decision-makers are also achievement-oriented but are less analytical in their thinking. They are comfortable with high information loads (cognitive complexity), but their people orientation means that their information collection methods may come through talking to people, especially to people who they see as experts. They tend to take a longer-term perspective and to be more creative than more analytical people.

4 Behavioural

Behavioural decision-makers have a strong people orientation. They generally communicate easily, using simple and understandable messages (low cognitive complexity), and make efforts to express interest in the well-being of others. They consult a great deal, are open to suggestions, are happy to compromise, and prefer a looser sense of leadership control. They do not feel the need to own decisions; they prefer decisions to be owned by everybody.

Ask yourself: What kind of decision-maker are you? What kind of decision-makers are your international partners? How far do you need to adapt your decision-making style to work more effectively with your international partners?

LEADING DECISION-MAKING MEETINGS

There are four key stages in a decision-making meeting that you need to manage effectively.

1 GETTING STARTED

When people work together over longer periods, there is less need to explain what a meeting is and how it should work. But with culturally diverse teams, it is useful for the chairperson to adopt a more explicit and structured approach to ensure that the purpose of the meeting, and the decision-making process, are clear.

Stage in an introduction to a meeting

Look at the following extract from the start of a meeting which uses clear and simple international English. What can you identify as the main stages in this introduction (e.g. welcome, introduce agenda)? You can then check your answer against the one in the Answer key at the back of the book. How useful would this style of introduction be for your international meetings? What things would you say differently if you were speaking to native speaker colleagues? Which of the main building blocks would you not use?

> OK, shall we get started? First, a quick welcome to Jan, who has joined us from the Belgian office. Nice to have you here. Jan will be presenting some figures later when we talk about the new cross-border initiative. OK, in terms of agenda, if you all have it in front of you, as you can see, the main objective today is to take a decision on the next phase of the project. Do we feel ready to start, and, if so, when? We'll do an update of progress so far, that's from me. Then I just want to give you some information from the recent leadership meeting in Milan. And then we can talk about the decision, and the pros and cons of moving on with things now or waiting. Just to remind you of a few rules, as always: mobile phones off, and the native English speakers should try to speak clearly so that our colleagues from around the world can understand. OK? Good, then let's get started with . . .

2 FACILITATING GROUP DISCUSSION

Once the introductions are over, and the purpose and process have been clarified, the next challenge is to manage the discussion. 'Facilitation' refers to a set of communication techniques used to manage group discussions. The chairperson is usually seen as the facilitator, but the efficiency and effectiveness of the discussion can be improved a lot if everyone uses facilitation skills. Some international leaders like to use external facilitators so that they, as leaders, do not dominate and so risk reducing the creativity of their team.

There are a number of key tasks that the facilitator needs to perform.

Stimulate the discussion

The first step towards a decision is to encourage participants to think creatively about possible solutions. Questions are the key here, and there are a number of different types that can be used which should be clear for both native and non-native English speakers.

- Questions to suggest a process: *Can we brainstorm a few ideas to begin?*
- Questions to invite opinions: *Sylvie, what do you think?*
- Questions to evaluate ideas: *Which of these ideas is most interesting for us?*
- Questions to stimulate alternatives: *Can we have some other views on this?*
- Questions to check direction: *So, what is our next step?*

Create the right atmosphere

The facilitator should manage the emotional temperature to support decision-making. Ideas flow faster when the atmosphere is good and people feel relaxed. Praise and positive feedback can be used to create a feel-good factor. However, since the practice of feedback differs so much across cultures, facilitators need to use different styles to meet individual and cultural needs. Here are some examples with an explicitly positive feel.

- Using quality words (to satisfy feelings): *Thanks for that idea. It's a **great** suggestion.*

- Using process words (to satisfy the intellect): *Good. I think this has been very **efficient**.*

Clarify

It is often difficult for non-native speakers of English to follow and understand a complex discussion. The facilitator should ensure, as far as possible, that everything is clear for everyone. This can be done in two main ways.

- Focus on surface-level clarity. This means clarifying the meaning of what is said: *If I understand you correctly, you mean …*
- Focus on deep-level clarity. This means clarifying the motivation or assumptions behind the words: *Why do you say that? Do you feel that … ?*

Good facilitators ask questions like these even when they themselves are sure of the answers, if they believe it helps others in the group.

Keep control

The facilitator has to watch the time. Reminding people of the agenda and pushing people to move on are also important functions, although it is necessary to be sensitive to the different priorities that people give to schedules.

Ensuring balanced participation – so that everyone has a chance to speak – is another part of the facilitator's role. Personality and cultural factors can affect the participation styles of different members: facilitators may need to work hard to encourage quieter, more introverted people to take part, and to make sure that talkative extroverts do not talk too much.

- Encouraging quiet people: *Harald, what do you think? It would be good to hear your ideas.*
- Controlling talkative people: *Sorry to interrupt, Valerie, but can we hear from Harald first, please?*

Summarise

Frequent summarising helps to create common understanding, and provides opportunities to reflect and comment on what has been said, and on the process. Some facilitators like to take responsibility for summarising. Others delegate this to group members who do it well. Allowing break-out groups for non-native speakers to summarise the meeting in their own language can also be helpful.

- Summarising the discussion: *So, we have discussed a number of issues today.*
- Summarising the process: *I thought the discussion was excellent at the beginning, but we must make sure that we listen carefully to everybody.*

3 OPTIMISING DIVERSITY

International meetings can be very diverse in terms of general outlook (analytical/creative), attitudes to decision-making (hierarchical/egalitarian), communication styles (direct/indirect), language level, and so on. Facilitators can use these three strategies to deal with this challenge.

Norming

Defining a clear process and clear communication rules is one way to manage differences in attitude, communication style and language level. Here are three examples of such rules.

- Everyone should have the opportunity to say something at the meeting.
- The chairperson has the right to interrupt people who talk for too long.
- The chairperson should invite quieter individuals to say something.

Linking

This means asking individuals explicitly to comment on each other's ideas.

- Connecting ideas: *Andres, what do you think about Brittany's point?*
- Directing questions to the group: *Can I ask Anna to answer your question, Jan?*

Linking forces people to listen to each other and engage with their ideas. This can develop mutual understanding and respect, and create a sense of teamwork and commitment towards the common target. It also slows communication down and allows those with a lower level of English to contribute.

Integrating

This means bringing together ideas to encourage a creative approach. It involves respecting different points of view, looking for compromise, and finding solutions by taking the best from the different perspectives.

- Identifying differences of opinion: *The major issue at the moment seems to be …*
- Respecting different positions: *OK, I think both these opinions are useful.*
- Exploring compromise: *If we were to …, could you …*
- Taking the best from the diverse perspectives: *John, if we take your point on cost saving and what Louise said about customer priorities, we could …*

Achieving synergy is the ultimate aim of facilitation. Diversity can seem to be a threat to group decision-making processes, but it also represents a great opportunity in terms of creativity and innovation.

4 MAKING THE DECISIONS

At some point, the talking has to stop and decisions have to be made. However, it can sometimes be difficult to move a group away from discussing ideas and towards actually taking a decision. Use these three steps.

1. Guide the discussion towards a decision.

2. Confirm the decision.

3. Agree who does what and by when.

Look at this extract from a meeting, in which you will see these three steps in action. Notice how very simple English which is clear to most non-native English speakers can be used to manage these important steps.

Fiona: *OK, we need to take a decision on this. We're running out of time. Marianne, do you agree to this?*

Marianne: *Yes.*

Fiona: *Good. And Frank, can you go with this?*

Frank: *Yes, that's fine with me.*

Fiona: *OK, this means we're deciding to open the new store at the end of the year, not in the middle as we originally planned. What we need to do now is look again at roles and scheduling. Marianne, what's your availability for the second half of this year? …*

5 CLOSING AND IMPLEMENTING

Despite all the hard work done to create a clear communication process and include everyone in the decision-making, many international meetings finish with participants unclear about what has been agreed, and they may be too embarrassed to admit this. Here is a six-step process for closing international meetings.

1. Confirm that all points have been discussed.

2. Summarise.

3. Check that the decisions are understood.
4. Repeat who is responsible for what and by when – make sure this is in the minutes.
5. Agree the date of the next meeting.
6. Close with positive comments on the outcome of the meeting.

Now read an extract from the close of a meeting. Which of the steps are included and which not? Notice how the chair makes positive comments about the success of the meeting in simple English. How important in your working context is it to celebrate success in this way?

OK, are there any other points we need to talk about today? No? Then perhaps I should sum up quickly and confirm the next steps. Basically, we've agreed to set up a pilot project to see if this is the right software for the company. And we've also suggested that Gill will head things up, although this needs to be confirmed with her line manager. The timeframe for completion is open and that's something to be discussed at the next meeting – pretty urgently in fact. Then in terms of actions, I need to talk to my boss and see if we can get a budget for this. Once that is confirmed, we can get together and start to define the project teams and sub-projects in more detail. That's in the minutes, Bob, yes? Good. Right, then I think we can finish there. Let me close by saying: great job! It was a difficult meeting in many ways but a great result, and I feel there's real commitment to this from everyone. Thank you!

6 MANAGING AND MONITORING DECISIONS

Decision-making really starts when the meeting stops. Effective international managers need to work hard to track the decisions taken in order to check that participants have understood them and are committed to doing what they said they would do. Without such tracking, the implementation of decisions will fall behind schedule as participants give time to other work priorities.

Think about what happens when decisions are made in your organisation. Are they always implemented as planned? What can you do to make sure you and others implement decisions effectively?

DECISION-MAKING STYLES

Differences in decision-making style can cause real challenges for professionals collaborating internationally. Take time to clarify how decisions will be taken, by whom and for what purpose. This will help you to work far more effectively.

CASE STUDY 2

'DIDN'T WE DECIDE THAT ALREADY?'

CASE STUDY 2

Read the case study which illustrates some of the challenges which occur when communicating internationally. Then answer the questions and compare your answers with the case commentary.

◇◇

'Didn't we decide that already?'

Paul Jacobs, a software specialist for a global pharmaceutical company based in Chicago, was a little confused. He normally enjoyed working in Europe but he had just got off the phone to his project leader, Karl Weiss, having had what he at best would call a curious conversation. Paul, Karl and the rest of the project team had been in Vienna at the beginning of the week to kick off a new European IT project, yet another roll out of corporate software to a subsidiary in Eastern Europe, this time Moldova. The discussion at the meeting had been rather difficult, trying to get everyone to agree on some pretty basic stuff, such as start date for implementation, quality KPIs (key performance indicators) and a provisional timing for the go-live. There had been a lot of discussion around possible risks – no one really knew the Moldovan business unit very well, and people were concerned about hidden problems.

The discussion had really dragged on for Paul who had only just managed to contain his frustrations. He was very much a doer and was quite happy to get started without pinning everything down first. If things were to go wrong, he knew he could put them right. This is what fifteen years of project experience had taught him. Eventually, after a lot of toing and froing, a decision was made to create a separate project workstream just looking at risk.

On the flight home from Vienna, Paul had had an idea. Why not involve a risk expert? There were several excellent people he knew in the US. These guys could take a look at the project plan, and possibly talk to people in the Moldovan business unit. This could generate really useful insights for the project team – it might even have an impact on the schedule and help planning. He telephoned Karl to talk about his idea but things did not go as expected.

> Paul: *So, Karl, I've had this idea to help sort out the risk problem in Moldova. What we could do is involve a couple of risk experts from the US, just on a pretty informal basis, to help us out to evaluate things a little. I know a couple of excellent guys.*
>
> Karl: *Paul, we took a decision at the recent meeting together. We're going to create a specific workstream. Jean-Paul will take charge of that. I don't understand.*
>
> Paul: *I know we discussed it but …*
>
> Karl: *We didn't discuss it. We took a decision.*
>
> Paul: *OK, we took a decision. Whatever, but it's not cast in stone. I just think we need to be creative. I had a quick word with the guys here and they said they can help. They actually did something similar on another project recently. You see what I mean?*
>
> Karl: *Paul, sorry, I don't. As I said, we took a decision. We're a team and we need to act as a team. It's not good if we start trying to change things behind the backs of colleagues. It's going to damage trust.*

The call ended shortly afterwards. Paul was frustrated. Karl was the one showing a lack of trust, not him. Karl was not showing any faith in his ideas. The idea to involve risk guys could clearly help the project but it was falling on deaf ears. Karl was inflexible. If things continued like this, it clearly meant that this was going to be a very difficult and very long project.

QUESTIONS

1. What differences in decision-making style created the lack of understanding between Paul and Karl?

2. What strategies did Paul use to persuade Karl to accept his idea? How successful was he?

3. How could Paul have introduced his ideas to Karl more persuasively?

4. What do you think of Paul's conclusions after his call with Karl? How else could he have reacted?

OVER TO YOU

Think about the important decisions you have to take with international colleagues at work.

1. How do differences in decision-making style create challenges for you?

2. Which strategies do you use to influence important decisions? How successful are you?

COMMENTARY

1. Karl seems to be working with a more consensus-based decision-making style, wanting to involve everyone in his team and use the meeting as a forum in which decisions are taken in an open way. Once a decision has been taken after careful deliberation, with consideration of all the risks, then this decision is largely binding.

Paul has a more entrepreneurial style. He prefers to work faster, tolerating minor mistakes in the interests of speed. He is also more of an individualist, and happy to come up with extra ideas outside formal get-togethers. He also enjoys working one-to-one with the project leader to innovate on an ongoing basis. Karl sees Paul's style as too individualistic, operating against his sense of team ethic and likely to damage trust in the team. Paul finds Karl's approach slow, lacking in creativity and showing little trust in Paul's ability to innovate.

2. Paul uses a series of arguments to persuade Karl. There is a logic to involving people with risk expertise to help deal with the risk dimensions of the project. Paul personally recommends the individuals, and also backs up his own opinion with feedback from the individuals themselves following a conversation in which they report that they have the experience to help. He also appeals to Karl's sense of creativity in order to help him to rethink the initial decision but Paul is totally unsuccessful in persuading Karl.

3. Paul should have introduced his ideas at the formal decision-making meeting with the whole team, having researched the availability of the individuals, their suitability as support and an awareness of any associated costs. He should also have prepared strong responses to likely counter-arguments offered by Karl and/or the rest of the team.

As he failed to do this, he needs to review the progress of the risk workstream and, if it fails to deliver what it needs to the project, use a review of project performance as an opportunity to introduce his idea.

Alternatively, he could persist with his suggestion and provide supporting evidence to strengthen his idea, for example, the likelihood of the current decision failing, proof of the expertise of the suggested risk experts. Paul should bear in mind his need to develop Karl's trust in any case if he is to be listened to.

4. Paul reacted negatively to the experience. He is jumping to conclusions about Karl's behaviour, and assuming the worst. Firstly, he should have tried to appreciate Karl's approach – slow and consensus-based decision-making has clear advantages in many situations.

Secondly, he should consider that possibly he is wrong and Karl is right. The workstream solution may be optimal. It has everyone's support and has established a clear approach to handling the risk issue. Effective international communicators seldom start from the principle that they are right and others are wrong.

And in terms of personal development, he should reflect on his own behaviours. Why was it that he was unable to make Karl listen? How could he have communicated differently to be more effective? How can he avoid becoming too emotional too quickly?

Resistance from others is difficult to accept sometimes but, on reflection, can offer an enormous learning experience.

9

INFLUENCING

*Character may almost be called the most effective
means of persuasion.*

Aristotle, Greek philosopher (384–322 BC)

The ability to influence other people is a vital skill in business. But as a result of various factors, such as increasing internationalisation and changes to organisational structures, it is also becoming more challenging.

Professionals increasingly work in complex international matrix structures with multiple amd often ambiguous reporting lines. They also work more and more in virtual project teams for which the key decision-makers – the sponsor and the project leader – may be located in other countries. In these situations, people find it more difficult than in the past to influence those with whom they work. To do so, they need new and smarter methods.

In this chapter we look at some of the skills involved in influencing others, and provide some practical techniques for you to use at work in future.

Before you read on, think about these questions:

1. What do you understand by the so-called 'top-down' and 'bottom-up' approaches to influencing?
2. Which influencing techniques are most effective for you?
3. How can you deal with people who say 'no'?

4. What is *personal branding* and how can you use it to influence your career development?

A QUESTION OF POWER

Our ability to influence others depends on many factors. One of the most important is power. If we hold power or authority over somebody, this greatly increases the chance that they will do what we want them to do.

Power can come from many sources. Many societies connect power to gender (usually but not always male) or age, with elders carrying more authority. In modern organisations, in spite of talk of empowerment, leaders keep the right to take most big strategic and operational decisions.

If you have authority in a particular situation, you can use a top-down 'push' approach. This involves telling someone what to do. Many purchasers enter negotiations with vendors using this approach, exerting pressure for lower prices and/or increased levels of service.

Most vendors, on the other hand, recognise their weaker position and use a bottom-up 'pull' approach. This involves creative questioning and effective listening in order to identify mutual needs that can be satisfied via a 'win-win' solution.

TECHNIQUES FOR INFLUENCING PEOPLE

As with all communication, influencing others has to be seen within a specific context. Something which persuades a person in one situation may fail completely in another. Here we look at eight dimensions of influencing others at work.

1 STRESS THE BENEFITS

People are more likely to be influenced by someone who offers something that satisfies their interests. These interests may be tangible, such as a salary increase or a more interesting job. Or they may be less tangible, like recognition or appreciation. Successful influencers are like detectives who find out what others need and then satisfy these needs in a way that is seen as supportive, not patronising.

Ask yourself: How far do you focus on asking people questions to find out their needs rather than telling them what you 'know' is good for them?

2 BUILD TRUST

People are more likely to be influenced by someone they trust (see Chapter 7). If I ask you to do something, and you trust that there is a good reason behind my request, there is a greater chance that you will agree. But how do we build trust? Three main ingredients in trust are:

- competence
- integrity
- empathy.

Showing these help you to build trust and, through this, to create opportunities to influence others.

Ask yourself: Do people know enough about you and your skills to trust in your judgement?

3 BE TRANSPARENT

People who explain their thinking openly, and who get their ideas across clearly, are more likely to be seen as convincing. In contrast, people who have difficulty expressing their ideas, and who cannot explain effectively the reasons behind their suggestions, may be seen as incompetent, or even manipulative.

Ask yourself: How far are you seen to be a clear communicator using understandable 'international' English?

4 USE LOGICAL ARGUMENTS

People find it hard to resist an argument built on logic and solid data. However, it is important to communicate the right level of information and analysis when building an argument because very complicated arguments can threaten and confuse some people.

Ask yourself: How far do people describe you as someone who uses logical arguments (without being too complex)?

5 FOCUS ON THE RELATIONSHIP

People are usually more open to being influenced by people they like or with whom they have something in common. This makes relationship-building and networking skills important, so you should invest time in developing personal relationships. Remember, however, that the speed and style of relationship building depends on psychological and cultural factors.

Ask yourself: Do you know how others view your attempts to influence them? How good are the relationships you have with key stakeholders? How do others value the relationship they have with you?

6 BE STRONG

People are more likely to be influenced by someone who communicates their ideas with energy and enthusiasm. If you do not seem convinced by your own arguments, why should others be? However, it is important to consider psychological and cultural factors here too. What is seen as powerful and assertive in some contexts could be seen as aggressive in cultures that value harmony.

Ask yourself: How far do others see the way you argue and persuade as being, on the one hand, assertive or, on the other hand, aggressive?

7 LOOK TO THE FUTURE

People who have a clear vision of the future, and who can explain clearly how they plan to realise this vision, are seen as more engaging and influential. Visions expressed in terms of a metaphor or story, rather than with facts and figures, may be more inspirational and effective.

Ask yourself: How far do others see you as inspirational and visionary?

8 SHOW OPTIMISM

Being negative is not usually inspiring. Positive thinkers, with energy and enthusiasm for creative solutions, are usually more appealing and influential. So try to persuade people by being more 'can do' than 'maybe not'. However, do not come across as being over-optimistic or over-positive, as people may see this as unprofessional.

Ask yourself: Do others see you as a positive or negative person?

STORYTELLING AS AN INFLUENCING TECHNIQUE

Storytelling is the most powerful way to put ideas into the world today. Robert McAfee Brown, theologian and peace campaigner (1920–2001)

A growing number of business leaders are learning storytelling skills to help them to influence their employees. Storytelling is an ancient skill that has informed, entertained and influenced people for thousands of years. Traditionally, oral stories were a means of transferring culture from one generation to another, creating a bridge between past and present. Today, business leaders tell memorable stories to inspire, influence and guide their employees through change, something that is often impossible with a simple explanation of facts and figures.

The use of personal anecdotes is one of the most common storytelling techniques. Anecdotes have the advantage of revealing the human side of the leader, connecting speaker and listener at an emotional level, with the audience experiencing reality through the eyes, ears and feelings of the storyteller. Here are four different types of anecdote that you can use to influence people.

AN INSIGHT INTO PERSONAL VALUES

Telling a short story about yourself – for example, how you faced a difficult choice or an embarrassing moment, or how you achieved an important success unexpectedly – can be a good way to talk about shared personal values and establish a basis for others to know and respect you.

A LEARNING EXPERIENCE

Sharing a learning experience, particularly if it is personal or even painful, can be a powerful way to support your proposals. Telling a story that shows how you initially made a mistake but then, with help, learned how to solve a problem similar to the challenge facing your organisation, is a powerful way of introducing a solution to a current problem.

A MOMENT OF CONFUSION

Telling a story about a misunderstanding you once experienced – either because you misunderstood someone or because they misunderstood you – can be a good way to challenge people's perceptions of a situation, to warn them against misunderstanding, or to ask them to look more deeply into an idea that, at first sight, they would reject.

A TALE OF PERSISTENCE

Telling a story of perseverance in the face of hardship and difficulty is a good way to raise spirits at difficult times and to motivate people to keep going. These stories tend to rely on anecdotes about famous historical or contemporary figures but can also work well if they touch on an element of your own life story.

TRY IT YOURSELF
Use each of the four storytelling formats to develop personal anecdotes that you can use in a range of professional contexts to persuade others.

DEALING WITH 'NO'

Your ability to influence others depends partly on your ability to prepare effective arguments. It also depends on your ability to deal with objections to your proposals, to be able to come up with effective responses when people say 'no' to your ideas. So try to anticipate objections and plan your counter-arguments. Below are several types of objection that are commonly made in discussions. What counter-arguments can you use? Note down your ideas. Can you think of any other types of argument that you might hear?

Type of objection	What is said	How to respond
Morality	*That isn't ethical.*	
Analysis	*We need more data.*	
Experience	*We've tried this before.*	
Priorities	*I have something else to do.*	
Fear of failure	*What if this goes wrong?*	
Ignorance	*I don't understand.*	
Power play	*I cannot accept this.*	
Fear of change	*I think many people will react negatively to the change.*	

INFLUENCING HOW PEOPLE SEE YOU

Influencing people is not limited to single issues, such as getting agreement on an agenda point in a meeting. Influence has much wider importance, especially if we think about how we should build our reputation and career inside a multinational organisation. Every time you walk into a room you create some kind of effect with the clothes you wear, your hairstyle, your smile, the way you speak and listen, the way you lead, and so on.

Some professionals find it helpful to think about their *personal branding*. There are consultancies which aim to help people to influence how they are seen by superiors, colleagues and clients in order to improve their career opportunities. Not everyone likes this approach, but if you decide to adopt it and try to interest others in your personal brand, you need both a clear product (what you are) and a promotional strategy (to make others aware of you). These three steps can help you to create your brand.

STEP 1: DEFINE YOUR USP

Your Unique Selling Proposition (USP) consists of the special features you offer, your unique value. Brands such as Pepsi, Nike and BMW spend millions on their USPs, but you have to do it less expensively! So think about what you can offer that makes you different from and valuable to the people around you at work. Use the questionnaire on page 120 to help you to describe your special value to others. Then write down a short brand statement for yourself, using fewer than 20 words, and read it aloud to yourself several times. What does this really say about you? Do you think others think about you in the same way? If not, you have a selling job to do.

STEP 2: PROMOTE YOURSELF

You may have wonderful qualities but if nobody in your organisation knows about them, then you are unlikely to maximise your potential. Successful branding is based on an effective communication strategy. This means promoting yourself internally to colleagues and management, as well as externally to customers. If you want to be seen to be valued, you need to take steps to become known – by getting invited to meetings, participating in extra projects, going to conferences, building new networks, and letting people know who you are and what you can do. The network that you build – friends, colleagues, clients and customers – will act as a promotional tool for your reputation and create career opportunities. It is important to get the balance right. In some cultures too much self-marketing can be extremely counterproductive.

STEP 3: ADD VALUE THROUGH VISIBLE LEADERSHIP

If you want to improve the value of your career brand, you have to take the initiative and show leadership potential as often as possible. This can include everything from taking the minutes in weekly staff meetings to volunteering to lead new projects. As you acquire additional responsibilities, your authority and reputation will grow, adding further to your brand image.

CHECK YOUR ABILITY TO INFLUENCE

So, are you a successful influencer? How well are you doing? You probably have a sense of your own success, but do you ask people around you about this? Getting feedback is the best way to discover how successful an influencer you really are. So why not ask a few trusted superiors, colleagues or customers about your personal style of influencing people? What can they tell you about your performance in meetings or your style of presenting? Getting this information will enable you to identify the strengths you can work on. And you may find a few weaknesses to work on too.

DEFINING YOUR PERSONAL BRAND

Use the questionnaire to think about your personal brand, to identify both strengths and weaknesses. You could also copy the questionnaire before you fill it in and give it to colleagues, superiors or friends to complete. Then compare your answers with theirs to help you develop a personal action plan.

Personal brand for (name):

What expertise do I offer my team?

What results do I guarantee management?

What levels of service do I offer to my customers?

What vision do I have for my staff?

What are my biggest strengths?

What are my most important weaknesses?

Which personal trait of mine is most valued by others?

What skills do I have that others do not?

My brand statement (maximum 20 words):

What should I do next to develop and promote my personal brand?

10

DEALING WITH 'DIFFICULT PEOPLE'

*Eventually we will find (mostly in retrospect, of course)
that we can be very grateful to those people
who have made life most difficult for us.*

Ayya Khema, German-born Buddhist nun (1923–97)

When communication breaks down and misunderstanding or conflict arises, we can be quick to label others as the reason for the problem: he does not listen, or she is not open. However, we may be looking at the problem in the wrong way. The difficulty may not be in others but more in ourselves.

In this chapter we look at how to manage people whom we see as difficult and how to manage our views on these people. We look at how to avoid communication breakdowns, and how to deal with them when they do happen.

Before you read on, think about these questions:

1. Why do we see others as difficult?
2. How can we communicate with others more openly?
3. How can we manage our impatience?
4. What are the advantages of working more closely with people we find difficult?

TOWARDS MORE OPEN COMMUNICATION

WHY DO WE SEE OTHERS AS DIFFICULT AND WHAT CAN WE DO ABOUT IT?

Dealing with our own prejudices is difficult. We each build a picture of the world that makes sense to us and helps us to live our lives. When someone else challenges this 'mental model', for example by wearing different clothes, having a different sense of humour, disagreeing very directly in a meeting, or organising a project in a different way, we often have a very basic reaction: to defend ourselves and attack the behaviour of the other.

This behaviour can be difficult to control but when communicating in culturally diverse international contexts we need to learn to recognise and manage this basic reflex.

THREE STEPS TO MORE OPEN COMMUNICATION

How can we learn to communicate with others more openly? First, we need to accept that nobody has a monopoly on the truth. There are many different ways of making sense of a complex world. So rather than defending our own view, we should start by consciously and regularly challenging our own ideas and opinions, particularly in situations when we become emotional and make negative judgements about other people.

Openness is especially important when working in multicultural environments because people's values and behaviours can be so different. If we become irritated or frustrated by those who do not do things our way, our communication is affected and we limit the ability to work with others effectively.

The solution is to think more about *how* we think, and then to select positive rather than negative communication behaviours. The three steps in this process are to:

1. recognise our negative interpretations of someone else's behaviour as they happen

2. remain open and analyse the possible meanings of the behaviour fairly in order to develop a more positive understanding

3. choose a positive communication strategy to deal with the behaviour based on this more positive analysis.

The tables on pages 123–125 give three cases of this three-stage process.

Recognising negative interpretation	Analysing another's behaviour fairly	Choosing a positive communication strategy
Case 1		
'This person is very arrogant. He loves the sound of his own voice. He talks far too much and dominates most of the meetings he is in. He doesn't listen and never asks other people what they think. He's really difficult to work with.'	'This person may be justifiably confident in his own expertise and thus believes he has the answers to most problems. It's possible that he sees his contributions as wholly constructive. He may believe that a good professional gives long and complete inputs in discussions. He may not have the necessary skills to summarise complex arguments in a simple way. He may ask few questions because he expects others to provide input if they have something they want to say, rather than to wait to be asked.'	'It could be useful to discuss ground rules for meetings to avoid domination by certain speakers. It could also be useful to find a polite and constructive way of interrupting this person. I may need in the short term to accept his communication style although I'll try and show him that it isn't always appreciated or helpful, and that we may both need to adapt to the style of the other in order to communicate successfully.'

Recognising negative interpretation	Analysing another's behaviour fairly	Choosing a positive communication strategy
Case 2		
'She's a poor leader. She doesn't know the jobs of the people she's managing. She never gives clear direction and she just expects others to solve problems on their own. She's weak. In meetings, she just listens and lets discussions go on and on.'	'This may be a case of uncertain leadership. It could be that she has a poor grasp of the management demands of her position and so does not provide clear direction. It could also be that she sees leadership more in terms of empowerment than directing. She may trust her employees to do their jobs properly and may want to encourage personal confidence and responsibility rather than dependence. Her listening style could be an expression of this.'	'One strategy could be to discuss the expectations that this manager has of her staff. If done in a constructive way, this could lead to better working practice. If she demands a different type of response from her team from the one they are giving, greater flexibility from team members may be necessary. If her behaviour is due to weaknesses in management knowledge or leadership skills, then the situation should be handled sensitively, although training and coaching may help.'

Recognising negative interpretation	Analysing another's behaviour fairly	Choosing a positive communication strategy
Case 3		
'She always seems to argue and become aggressive and competitive in discussions. She tends to criticise others and never sees that she may be partly responsible. She can never admit that she has made a mistake.'	'This could be someone who sees herself as having strong views on a subject on which she is an expert (which may be fully justified). She may also be able to separate the topic from the person in discussions. So while she may appear aggressive, she isn't being personal but simply interrogating the topic. It's also possible that her criticism of others hides insecurity about herself, which could need careful handling.'	'It's important to remain emotionally calm during discussions with combative individuals. Remember, such people can't make you angry themselves; anger is created by you losing emotional control. So I need to manage my emotions. If necessary, I can try and communicate to her in private the effect her behaviour is having on others. She may be unaware of the negative feelings she's generating and be open to change. It could also be helpful to clarify with her some ground rules for effective communication.'

MANAGING IMPATIENCE

The ability to move from interpretation (stage 2) to a more positive analysis and an effective communication strategy (stage 3) requires a lot of effort and emotional control. This is especially difficult for people who are under time pressure, because impatience often destroys opportunities to think in a more constructive way.

Although we sometimes connect impatience with positive values – our own efficiency or our ability to see the correct solution faster than others – it is actually a signal of our intolerance. Impatience can destroy relationships by sending messages of disrespect and distrust. This means it has to be managed as a matter of priority. Take the test to find out how impatient you are.

TEST: HOW IMPATIENT ARE YOU?

For each of the following statements, give yourself a score of between 0 (never impatient) to 5 (often impatient). Then add up your total score and look at the comments in the Answer key at the back of the book.

	Never impatient				Often impatient
I get impatient with people who ...	0 – 1 – 2 – 3 – 4 – 5				

1 talk too much in meetings.

2 reply to my emails with the wrong information.

3 tell me something that I already know.

4 do not accept an idea of mine that I know is good.

5 do not arrive at meetings on time.

6 cannot take decisions quickly.

7 are afraid to take a new direction.

8 do not understand what I tell them.

9 waste time with small talk.

10 think they know everything but really know nothing.

Total [   ]

Now let us look at how to manage impatience. There are two main steps in this process.

Know the causes

Start paying attention to what starts off your feelings of impatience. Is it how someone talks in a meeting? Is it a particular style of email? Are you more likely to be impatient in the morning or later in the day? Keep a diary of your reactions and look for patterns. Ask people who know you to describe how you look and what you say when you are impatient. This will help you to recognise and to control the emotion.

Learn self-control

Here are some thoughts and questions to help you to control your impatience.

1. Recognise that impatience can destroy effective communication. Do you want to be ineffective?
2. Remember that the only person who can make you feel impatient is you. The final responsibility for feeling impatient does not lie with anyone else, only with you.
3. If you start to feel impatient, 'step outside' the emotion as it rises inside you. Imagine watching yourself from a distance or putting the emotion in a box. At the same time, create a sense of calm by filling your mind with pleasant thoughts and memories. Try to control your breathing and posture. Re-engage with the other person and try to discover what is interesting or of value in what they are saying or doing.
4. Impatience is often generated when we feel that our agenda is not being followed or people are not listening to us. So forget your agenda and invest more time in understanding the other person's point of view. In discussion, avoid saying *Yes, but ...;* instead say *Why do you say that?*

As you begin to think more and engage with the other person, your negative feelings will decrease and you can try for more constructive dialogue.

TUF

Use the TUF approach –Time out, Understand, Framework – with people whom you find difficult. TUF is both *reflective* – asking you to analyse your own view of a situation – and *active* – suggesting things you might say or do at specific moments.

1 Time out

Take a time out and reflect on why you think someone is difficult. Ask yourself:

- What is this person actually doing that I find difficult?
- Why do I find this behaviour difficult?
- How would other people define this same behaviour?
- How would the person explain his/her own behaviour?
- What aspects of this person's behaviour may I be misinterpreting?
- What am I doing that makes the situation worse?
- What can I do to improve the situation?

2 Understand

The second step is to check your understanding of the motivation and meaning behind the other person's message.

3 Framework

The third step is to set a framework for effective dialogue.

FINAL THOUGHTS

Few of us get the chance to choose our colleagues and business partners, so there will always be people whom we find frustrating and situations that we find difficult. If we want more effective workplace relationships, the real challenge is to manage our basic human tendency to classify particular people and reactions as difficult.

Taking time to understand ourselves – our reactions, prejudices and fears – is a good starting point, although this can also be quite painful. We have to admit weakness and start learning from those who can really challenge us. If we can commit to this approach, we have an opportunity to reduce the potential for conflict and its impact in the workplace. And we can create a communication culture in which diversity produces real benefits for ourselves, others and our organisation.

11

MANAGING CONFLICT

A good manager doesn't try to eliminate conflict,
(s)he tries to keep it from wasting the energies of his (or her)
people. If you're the boss and your people fight you openly
when they think that you are wrong – that's healthy.

Robert Townsend, American business executive and author (1920–98)

The damage which conflict can cause is clear. Conflict can undermine relationships, reduce the motivation and creativity of individuals and teams, and lead to higher costs and lower productivity.

However, conflict also has benefits. Disagreements between individuals serve to reveal underlying organisational problems that need to be dealt with. Conflict in diverse, multicultural teams can help to avoid the problem of 'group think', when everyone thinks in the same way. And if conflict is managed successfully, people can achieve better levels of understanding, leading to better relationships and improved results.

Before you read on, think about these questions:

1. What does conflict mean to you?
2. What are the main causes of conflict?
3. Why does conflict arise in international teams?
4. How can you deal with conflict?

WHAT IS CONFLICT?

The term 'conflict' is used in a wide range of contexts and with different meanings. In politics, we talk about international conflicts caused by clashes of religious values, identities and historical perspectives. At the other end of the scale, a minor disagreement in a meeting can be called a conflict of opinion. There are also conflicts of interest in business, when there is an important difference between someone's individual interests and the interests or values of their organisation.

In order to better understand conflict, think about the differences between conflict, misunderstanding and disagreement.

Conflict and misunderstanding

Conflict begins when people have opposing interests – when one person stops another from reaching a goal. In organisations, there can be conflict about anything, from booking a meeting room to major disputes over company strategy. But a misunderstanding is not necessarily a conflict. When you deal with a misunderstanding, you may find that you and the other person actually have shared interests. This is why understanding how others see a situation is so important during conflict resolution: there may be enough underlying common interest to solve the problem quickly.

Conflict and disagreement

Conflict involves emotions: it can make people feel irritated, frustrated, angry or upset. Disagreements, on the other hand, do not necessarily involve emotions. They can be quite cool and rational: disagreements are simply differences of opinion. In conflict, it is often people's emotions that are the real challenge because they radically reduce our ability to act rationally and constructively. Problematically, what counts as a disagreement in one culture may be seen as a conflict in another. This has the potential to generate huge misunderstandings.

Remember: Understanding and managing one's own feelings are critical to dealing with conflict successfully.

CAUSES OF CONFLICT

There are a number of causes of conflict. These often happen together to make the conflict more complex and more difficult to resolve. Two key causes of conflict at work are organisational change, and a lack of understanding of team dynamics.

ORGANISATIONAL CHANGE

Globalisation is causing dramatic changes to the way companies work. One example is the standardisation and centralisation or outsourcing of functions like IT and finance. These processes can increase the tensions that already exist between people working in the head office, who may struggle to maintain their authority, and people in subsidiaries, who may struggle to maintain their autonomy.

The global pressure to be competitive produces frequent restructuring, with employees facing big and often unwelcome changes to the way they work and to their responsibilities. They may need to work on change projects on top of their normal line responsibilities. And this means an increased workload, which is a further source of stress and conflict.

Managers who lead change internationally need to find the time to meet people face to face in different countries. They need to provide a clear and engaging vision that supports employees through difficult change processes, which may be far from transparent or logical. Unfortunately, leaders often communicate poorly in such situations, and they make two main mistakes.

Insufficient communication

People working internationally often do not communicate enough with their colleagues: this can create big problems in international projects. For example, team members often struggle as it emerges over time that individuals are not really competent to complete a task or that they cannot fulfil a commitment because of the objections of a local senior manager – something not apparent at the outset. Good international operators avoid these conflicts by getting to know their colleagues and their local contexts better, and by checking frequently whether agreed actions are achievable.

Insensitive communication

Working internationally demands new sensitivities. We have to recognise that communicating in our usual way – which we may consider natural, honest and open – may itself be a source of conflict. Our communication style may be confusing or offensive to others. For example, communicators who place a high value on directness, objectivity and what they see as an honest search for the truth, may be seen as rude, aggressive or uncultivated in cultures with a preference for more indirect communication. Likewise, indirect communicators may be seen as lacking focus or as evasive by more direct communicators.

Remember: Clear speaking, effective listening and giving useful feedback all help to build mutual understanding and to reduce the chances of conflict.

TEAM DYNAMICS

Another common source of conflict is a lack of understanding of how teams work. Understanding the dynamics of teams involves understanding team processes and team roles. Americans Bruce W. Tuckman and Mary Ann Jensen believe that teams go through a number of stages of development, one of which – the 'storming phase' – involves conflict.

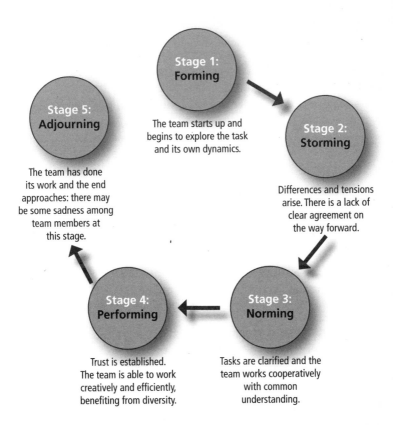

If we understand that the life of a team often develops in this way and that storming is an inevitable and even necessary phase of team development, then conflict will seem less threatening and more of a natural process that can be managed by techniques such as:

- sensitising the team to the storming phase
- stressing the value of diversity
- establishing rules early to manage conflict.

Managing diversity is critical to the good functioning of international teams. A number of psychometric models claim that teams can benefit from the right mix of different types of people doing different tasks. Knowing our own work and communication styles, and those of our international colleagues, can help us to appreciate others and to adapt our behaviour to a style more appreciated by others.

Remember: More and more international leaders believe that profiling team members, using a psychometric tool like Myers Briggs or TMS (see below) when the team first forms, is an effective way to support mutual understanding and to avoid or help to resolve conflicts.

WHO AM I? WHO ARE YOU?

The Team Management System, developed by Team Management Systems International Ltd, identifies eight common types of working style based on people's preferences in relation to the way they relate to others, the way they organise themselves and others, the way they process information, and the way they make decisions. TMSDI calls one of the types *Thruster-Organisers*. These are people who:

- like to organise and implement
- are quick to decide and are result-oriented
- set up systems
- are analytical
- make things happen
- take action by giving deadlines
- can put pressure on others
- may overlook people's feelings.

More managers fall into this category than any other. And although such people may bring a sense of dynamism and focus to teamwork, they can irritate team members who like more time to reflect. To such colleagues, the *Thruster-Organiser* may appear to be pushy and impatient. So to avoid conflict within teams, *Thruster-Organisers* who understand team dynamics try to adapt their communication style, for example by speaking more slowly, giving others more time to express their views, and stating clearly that these views are valued.

Ask yourself: Are you a *Thruster-Organiser?* What could you change to make it easier for others to work with you?

CULTURE AND PERSONALITY

Cultural difference is often put forward as another cause of conflict. Much has been written about how different attitudes to, for example, time, hierarchy or structure may lead to conflict. In fact, our attitudes towards these dimensions may be due to our personalities as much as to our cultural backgrounds. But they can still cause difficulties. Sometimes it can be little things like the tone of someone's voice or someone's sense of humour that create tensions between people. In such situations, we need to remember two things. First, as Stephen R. Covey, the management author and speaker, says, 'Strength lies in differences, not similarities'. Second, we should try to understand that being irritated by other people is not the result of their failings but of ours. Irritation, impatience and anger towards others usually say more about the limits of our own tolerance than about the qualities of others.

Remember: One of the most important skills in diversity management is being able to interact positively with people whom you may not feel very positively about.

DEALING WITH CONFLICT

There are many ways of dealing with conflict. The approach you use will depend on the specific people and situation. And you need to choose your strategy carefully. For example, if you do not have the necessary authority, you may not even have the right to challenge another person. Five possible strategies for dealing with conflict are shown in the diagram on page 138.

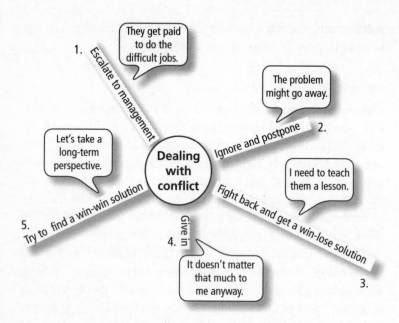

THE WIN–WIN APPROACH TO CONFLICT CONVERSATIONS

The choice of format for dealing with conflict is also wide, ranging from an informal one-to-one meeting over coffee to a more formal mediation or arbitration process involving external parties. Here we look at how you might handle a fairly formal meeting with members of your department or team.

Preparing for the meeting

You need to do some preparatory work to ensure that a resolution is reached in the face-to-face discussion. You should:

- establish the facts of the case, including claims and counter-claims
- understand any legal issues involved
- research the feelings and needs of the participants
- set clear goals for the meeting in advance in writing
- plan what to say if people get emotional.

Starting the meeting

It is important to create a professional and positive atmosphere quickly. You also need to establish clearly the purpose and the process of the discussion. So:

- open positively
- express your hope that a solution can be found
- state clearly the need to show respect for others
- clarify the agenda and timetable
- negotiate a process.

Should you present your views first or let others speak? Talking first can be helpful to stop others using negative arguments at the start. On the other hand, showing empathy by listening first may bring a resolution faster.

Managing the meeting

Emotions can run high when discussing a conflict. This makes it difficult to keep people thinking constructively. Here are some ideas to keep the dialogue solution-oriented.

- Keep the atmosphere positive.
- Leave more difficult items until later.
- Be polite.
- Let people give their views.
- Acknowledge other people's feelings.
- Minimise loss of face for all.
- Give positive feedback.

Closing the meeting

At the end of the meeting, summarise any agreement and finish on the right note, looking forward and not back.

- Summarise the agreement and clarify responsibilities for the next steps.
- Set a timetable for reviewing the next steps to ensure that they are implemented.
- Take time to celebrate success and reaffirm working relationships.

MANAGING CONFLICT IN MEETINGS

Answer these questions to give yourself feedback on your ability to manage conflict in meetings.

How well did I do on the following points?
(1 is the top mark and 6 is the lowest.)

	1	2	3	4	5	6
Was I prepared?	○	○	○	○	○	○
Was I clear?	○	○	○	○	○	○
Was I flexible?	○	○	○	○	○	○
Was I creative?	○	○	○	○	○	○
Was I positive?	○	○	○	○	○	○
Was I determined?	○	○	○	○	○	○
Was I persuasive?	○	○	○	○	○	○
Was I fair?	○	○	○	○	○	○
Was I successful?	○	○	○	○	○	○

What will I do differently next time?

Total [   ]

Photocopy this feedback form so that you can use it more than once.

Self-assessment

The final phase of the meeting happens when it is over. Take a few minutes to write down what you thought went well and what you might do differently in the future. Use the feedback form on page 140 to help you. This kind of exercise can help you to improve your performance next time.

BUILD, DON'T DESTROY

Conflict brings with it some opportunities and many risks. If we allow ourselves to become over-emotional in conflict situations, we may put our professional reputation and career at risk. Damaging relationships may limit our ability to deliver results in the future. So focus your energies on building good relationships and dealing with any conflicts that may arise when they arise.

12

GIVING AND GETTING FEEDBACK

Feedback is the breakfast of champions.

Ken Blanchard, American author and management guru (1939–)

Feedback is everywhere in business. Companies ask customers if they are pleased with their services. Participants fill out evaluation forms ('happy sheets') after training courses. Managers and staff take part in appraisal interviews. Colleagues give each other informal feedback during conversations round the coffee machine.

The goal of feedback is simple: to improve performance. Feedback can help individuals and organisations to learn from the past and to develop competitive advantages in the future. Feedback helps people to think about their strengths and to identify areas to work on. Feedback can be central to the success of an organisation.

In this chapter we focus on some of the key aspects of more formal manager-report feedback, although many of the ideas can also be applied to more informal everyday feedback conversations.

Before you read on, think about these questions:

1. Why do we give feedback?
2. How is feedback influenced by culture and by personality?
3. What are the key skills for giving feedback?
4. What are the key skills for receiving feedback?

5. What kind of feedback is it possible to give to international colleagues by email?

WHY DO WE GIVE FEEDBACK?

Feedback has three main objectives.

1. The objective of *developmental feedback* (also called *constructive feedback*) is to help people to develop and to become more effective. It is a basic responsibility of any manager to give this kind of feedback. It means looking at performance and skills levels, and providing constructive guidance to individuals and groups on how to improve. Without such feedback, employees will probably fail to develop as fast and as far as they can.

2. *Affirmative feedback* simply means telling people that they did a good job. This explicit praising can satisfy an emotional need for recognition, and boost motivation and performance. Without praise, many employees become frustrated and demotivated.

3. With motivated employees who are developing skills and realising their potential, both kinds of feedback help organisations to work better.

FEEDBACK AND CULTURE

Culture relates to feedback in two main ways. First, feedback styles are influenced by culture. Second, it is the responsibility of leaders to create a 'feedback culture' in their international teams, departments or organisations.

BEING SENSITIVE TO CULTURE

Certain styles of feedback tend to be associated with certain national or organisational cultures. For example, a more direct form of feedback is often said to be preferred in some northern European business cultures, whereas in other parts of the world an indirect style is said to reflect a preference for harmony.

Attitudes to risk and quality may also influence the style of feedback in an organisation. Some organisations suffer from a 'blame culture' in which mistakes are not tolerated and strong criticism is voiced. This kind of environment makes openness and constructive feedback more difficult.

In very hierarchical organisations, feedback often only goes in one direction, namely from the top down. In collectivist or group-oriented environments, praising one individual may not be appropriate, and feedback is usually delivered to the whole team.

There are no rights or wrongs in this area. Direct feedback may sometimes work more effectively than softer and more polite indirect feedback – it all depends on the context. Managers need to be culturally sensitive and flexible.

Ask yourself: How effectively can and do you adapt your feedback style to different cultural contexts? Ask someone with a different cultural background from you to give you informal feedback on the way different people see your style.

CREATING A FEEDBACK CULTURE

People working in international teams and organisations need to create a common understanding about how they are going to work together. One way to do this is to discuss expectations and define team rules. For example:

- No interrupting people during meetings.
- Acknowledge emails within 24 hours, and deal with them within three working days.
- No escalation of problems to local management without internal team discussion first.

During this 'forming' process, team leaders and members can establish a culture in which constructive feedback is frequently asked for and openly given.

Feedback is particularly important as a way of dealing with misunderstandings among people with different values, expectations and behaviours. Team leaders should model the style of feedback they wish to create, and should discuss this with their project deputies. These sub-project heads will then feel more confident about giving feedback to their team members, who may also be inspired to give peer-to-peer feedback.

It is particularly important to clarify what feedback can be given by email. A simple rule of thumb is to use email only for giving constructive feedback. Any developmental feedback is best handled by telephone or face to face in order to handle things more sensitively.

In this way a feedback culture begins to develop. But to maintain the feedback culture, team leaders need to make sure that team members know how to give and to listen to feedback. This may require training at an early stage in the team's formation.

To help you to create a positive feedback culture, discuss these questions in your team:

Why? What are the main objectives of feedback? Are there any areas in which feedback will be especially useful?

How often? Is feedback to be given only once a year, at a formal appraisal interview, or will it be an informal, daily process?

Who? Who should give feedback? Is it a top-down process only, or can it also be bottom-up, with employees giving feedback to their managers? Is peer-to-peer feedback encouraged?

How? Does everyone have the same expectations? Do those receiving feedback just want some praise, or are they interested in learning how to improve? What style of feedback will be most effective with each member of the team?

Where? Is feedback to be given individually and privately, or openly, for example in team meetings? Is information exchanged during feedback confidential, or can it be communicated to others in the organisation?

Ask yourself: How can you help to create a feedback culture within the group that you work in?

PERSONALITY AND FEEDBACK

National and organisational factors influence how feedback is given and received, but personality has a big impact too. People vary enormously in how open they are to receiving feedback, and in their capacity for personal change. You must think about this before you decide on both the content and the style of the feedback which you want to give someone. Sensitive managers tune into the people in front of them, and use different feedback styles in different situations.

Ask yourself: How far do you fine tune your feedback style to suit different individual personalities?

HOW TO GIVE FEEDBACK

Giving and receiving feedback are key responsibilities and key skills for every leader. Here are 11 tips to help you give developmental feedback.

1 Get the timing right

Feedback is best given as soon as possible after a particular event (although let the person receiving the feedback share in deciding the best time and place). Make sure that there is enough time to talk things through: different opinions may make the discussion longer.

2 Structure the meeting

Ideally, feedback is asked for rather than imposed, so if you are giving feedback to a direct report, you need to manage the process with special care. It is essential to be clear about your general intention, for example *I'd like to give you a little feedback about ...* , and about the positive motivation behind your feedback, for example *I think this can help you to ...* . This helps to ensure that employees remain open to the opportunity for development.

3 Start by listening

Encourage employees to assess themselves so that you can build on their own personal insights. People are often more willing to accept developmental feedback when they recognise their own strengths and weaknesses. In this phase it is important to listen. Do not give your own opinion too soon, but instead ask questions to encourage reflection and discussion. Rather than saying *I don't think anyone was very happy with the way you led the meeting*, you could ask *How did you feel about the meeting? How do you think other people felt about it?*

4 Comment, don't evaluate

One key feedback skill is to comment neutrally on the behaviour you have observed, rather than to offer (negative) interpretations or judgements. For example, saying *Your first input to the meeting took ten minutes* is more likely to encourage discussion than saying *You dominated the meeting*. Focus on specific facts and encourage employees to make their own assessments.

5 Talk about impact

Encourage employees to think about their impact on other people, for example by asking a question like *If you make a presentation in this way in front of clients, do you think there is a danger that ... ?* Often the impact of our behaviour is not what we intended, so we need to become aware of the impact that our behaviour could have, and to think about alternatives.

6 Look at perception gaps

It is very helpful to contrast the way we see ourselves with the way others see us. But we need to choose our language carefully so that we do not give people negative labels. For example, do not say *You are very dominant and people don't like that*, but rather *You may see yourself as a strong person. Others might see this behaviour as rather aggressive*. The use of *may* and *might* encourages people to see themselves through the eyes of others.

7 Explore alternatives

Help individuals to reflect on what they could do differently. During this phase, give people time to reflect on your feedback and to consider another way of doing things. Allow for periods of silence during this phase and treat these as positive: it means that the person you are giving feedback to is thinking about what you are saying!

8 Offer realistic suggestions

Sometimes you will need to suggest alternatives but try to build on suggestions which come from the employee. Be specific about how the individual can improve. Stress that the objective is to change behaviour, not personality. Make people aware that behavioural change takes time and needs commitment.

9 Be sensitive to resistance

Individuals can feel threatened by feedback. People with low self-esteem tend to hear only the negative messages. People with high self-esteem may hear only the positive messages. So observe and listen carefully to check that the feedback has been received as you intended.

10 Summarise and agree on a plan

If you are giving feedback to a report, summarise the objective and outcome of the feedback clearly in order to get commitment to measurable actions. Agree on a process to track progress and make sure the plan is implemented. End on an optimistic note to motivate the person further.

11 Get feedback on your feedback

Ask people what they valued about the conversation so that you can improve your skills. If we offer feedback, it is important that we are open to feedback ourselves.

A FOUR-PHASE PROCESS FOR GIVING FEEDBACK

Here is a model which shows four different phases for feedback.

Step 1	Step 2	Step 3	Step 4
Set up and begin the feedback meeting with a clear objective.	Describe and discuss behaviours and the impact of behaviours.	Agree an action plan of which behaviours to change or to develop.	Summarise the feedback meeting and decide when next to meet.

HANDLING PEOPLE WHO DO NOT WANT FEEDBACK

Some people hear feedback as criticism and defend themselves by rejecting observations and blaming the situation or other people. Here are some ideas for handling these 'difficult' people.

Reflect on your authority to give feedback

Feedback can fail if the person giving it is not respected. For example, they may be seen as too young, too junior or the wrong gender in the eyes of the person receiving feedback. If your feedback is not working, think about how the other person may view your right to provide feedback.

Point out any unconstructive behaviour as it happens

If someone is interrupting, being defensive and generally not listening, it may be necessary to tell them that you feel that the way they are listening – or not listening – is not helpful.

Challenge people who over-simplify the solution

Some people claim to be flexible, and suggest it will be easy for them to change their behaviour. (*Sure, I'll speak more slowly at the next meeting so that people can understand. No problem.*) It may be necessary to insist on further meetings to review progress.

Make clear the consequences of people's behaviour

This can help to make people think again about the way they behave. For example, you could say *If you continue to talk over people during our meetings, I may have to ask you to stop talking altogether because it's making other people angry.* This gives people a simple choice: continue their behaviour and create a negative impact, or adapt and create a more constructive atmosphere.

Challenge people to be better team players and leaders

Highly talented and task-oriented individuals may not be very open to feedback. They are successful, so why should they change? In cases like these, it may be helpful to appeal to teamwork, stressing the importance of collaboration and the need to engage others.

GIVING FEEDBACK TO YOUR BOSS

Managers tend to get less feedback than anyone else, and some senior managers think that they are successful enough not to need any feedback. Only in flatter business cultures do leaders normally receive input from employees in upward appraisal interviews. Yet feedback to leaders can be extremely valuable for an organisation. Here are three tips.

1 Select the right strategy

Some managers are happy to hear straight talking from staff members; others need more sensitive handling. You may need to ask permission to give feedback. If giving upward feedback is not possible, you may want to involve another person who has the trust or authority to handle this conversation.

2 Focus on impact

Concentrate on the effect of the leader's behaviour on you or others, not on the intention behind the behaviour. When people feel challenged, they often start to defend themselves. Focus on specific things that were said and done, and show how they generated negative feelings among staff members.

3 Stress efficiency

Leaders may be persuaded to do things differently if they think this will improve results. Point it out if the leader's behaviour has damaged motivation, and stress the tangible results that can be achieved by alternative behaviours.

HOW TO RECEIVE FEEDBACK

Feedback helps us do better next time, but if our performance was not very good the first time, then we may not enjoy receiving feedback on a failure or a weakness. Yet to improve, we have to understand how others see us. So first, we need to think about which aspect of our performance (for example, our leadership, listening or technical skills) we would like feedback on. Then we need the courage to ask for feedback from others.

Feedback can be hard to take sometimes. It can feel like a criticism. We may even feel it is wrong, misguided or unfair. However, feedback is always useful information about how other people see us and the situation. We need to understand that opinion and be able to learn from it, and even change what we are doing if necessary. To understand feedback, we must be able to listen. Here are some ideas for improving your listening skills when you receive feedback.

Listen patiently

Do not interrupt. Stay cool, even when there is criticism.

Listen curiously

Do not defend yourself. Clarify the feedback with follow-up questions.

Listen actively

Reformulate what the person says to check that you have understood.

Listen concretely

Ask for specific examples of your behaviour to help you understand.

Listen positively

Give positive feedback to the speaker to encourage him/her to say more.

Listen physically

Maintain eye contact and use the right body language to show interest in the feedback.

Listen developmentally

Admit mistakes and ask for ideas on what you could do differently.

Listen creatively

Discuss your own ideas for what you could do differently.

Listen pragmatically

The objective of feedback is to change, so aim for a practical action plan.

Listen continually

Make sure you get ongoing feedback to check if you are developing.

Listening is hard work, particularly when we hear things that we do not like. So after feedback, you can also ask for feedback on your listening skills to check how open you were.

FEEDBACK WHICH MAKES A DIFFERENCE

Managers and coaches who spend a lot of time giving feedback to people working in international teams sometimes hear people say *Oh, yes. I've had this feedback before.* A good reply to this is *Fine. Try to make it the last time you hear it.*

Changing our behaviour is difficult and we often overestimate our ability to behave differently. The only way to know whether or not we have acted successfully on feedback is, of course, to get more feedback. If we keep getting the same feedback over a long period, we may find that we need a coach to help us move forward in a more structured and organised way.

But generally, getting regular feedback from our colleagues – peers, reports and managers – and customers, can be such a powerful way to improve performance that when we look back over a period of getting good feedback, we can be amazed at how far we have travelled.

FEEDBACK SELF-ASSESSMENT

How good do you feel you are at giving and receiving feedback? Make a list of your strengths and weaknesses, and think of suggestions for an action plan to improve your performance.

Self-assessment: giving feedback

My strengths

My weaknesses

My action plan

Self-assessment: receiving feedback

My strengths

My weaknesses

My action plan

CASE STUDY 3

'YOU WANT US TO DO WHAT?!'

CASE STUDY 3

Read the case study which illustrates some of the challenges which occur when communicating internationally. Then answer the questions and compare your answers with the case commentary.

◇◇◇

'You want us to do what?!'

Katie Pearson was a geologist working for a relatively small consulting company. She was well known in her field with over thirty years of experience in 'seek and find' exploration projects. One year ago her relatively small specialist company had become part of a major international project in the Gulf of Mexico, working with a number of global players in the industry to discover new oil fields. The scale of the project was new to Katie and her internal team, and although things had started on a high, they soon began to get difficult. AREMCO, a major player in oil and gas production, and overall project leader, had insisted on introducing its own project management approach but with documentation. Template after template crossed Katie's desk which she had to fill with information on her own company's working routines and results. Phone call after phone call followed asking for further information, questioning the validity of the information supplied, and introducing new requests at the last minute. She and her internal team were exhausted. There was never a word of thanks. There was always a climate of suspicion. For Katie, it seemed that AREMCO did not believe that she and her company could deliver. Then she received a request for her and her colleagues to work at the weekend to provide 'vital data' for the project. It was the last straw. She picked up the phone to talk to Janek, her contact in AREMCO:

Katie: *Janek, this is ridiculous. It's Friday morning and you're asking people here to suddenly work at the weekend. We keep getting these demands out of the blue.*

Janek: *Out of what?*

Katie: *From nowhere. I mean, it all feels chaotic. Your people are being disrespectful. My team are really demotivated. There's a real sense here that AREMCO doesn't trust our people with all these template requests and this constant checking.*

Janek: *Katie, this is normal for this kind of project. You've had a training course on AREMCO project management. You know the approach we take ... the documentation we need for our systems.*

Katie: *But we're spending more time on the documentation than on the actual project. It feels totally inefficient. And no one here feels that there's any respect.*

Janek: *It's not a question of respect. We need the data for our systems, not because we don't respect you.*

Katie: *But these last minute requests. People have family commitments.*

Janek: *We've got people working around the clock in our offices here. I'm asking your team to come into the office on Saturday for three hours. Is that really too much?*

Katie: *It's the attitude, Janek. We're fed up with the attitude here.*

Janek: *What? Sorry, I didn't get that. Look, let's talk at lunchtime. I have to go to a meeting now. I'll call you later.*

Katie: *As you wish.*

Katie was actually no wiser and certainly no happier after the call. It was impossible to get Janek to understand. She decided to set up an emergency meeting with her company director to brief him on the situation and ask advice on how best to handle the later call with Janek.

QUESTIONS

1. How far do you think Katie's frustrations were justified?

2. How effectively do you think she handled the telephone call?

3. How clear was Katie's use of English for Janek, a non-native speaker?

4. What do you think of Katie's decision to seek advice from her senior manager?

5. How else could Katie have dealt with this issue?

OVER TO YOU

Conflicts, especially those leading to breakdowns in trust, can represent a serious problem for those collaborating internationally.

1. Which conflicts do you experience when communicating internationally? Which approaches are successful in solving these conflicts?

2. Which behaviours in a business context do you find disrespectful? Which of these behaviours arise from cultural differences?

3. How might your own behaviours come across to international colleagues as disrespectful? What can you do to ensure that this does not happen?

COMMENTARY

1. Katie's frustrations were entirely natural. In fact, it is common for those working in smaller companies to experience the more structured data reporting systems used by larger organisational partners to be overly bureaucratic. It is also possible that Katie and her internal team were unused to the volatility and unpredictability of large projects. However, the frustrations are not wholly justified as AREMCO provided training in its systems, which should have prepared Katie and her internal team for new working processes. If the training was not adequate, she should have communicated her concerns earlier, which could have avoided the level of conflict which occurred during the telephone call.

2. Effectiveness is difficult to measure from a single phone call. In one sense it is effective as the problem is now out in the open, feelings have been vented and there is an opportunity in the next call to find a way forward. In terms of the specific call, Katie does not use very constructive strategies.

She uses strong terms which Janek experiences as inflammatory: *ridiculous, chaotic, totally inefficient*

She labels the behaviours of other people, ascribing negative motives:
Your people are being disrespectful.

She contradicts rather than listens:
But …

She does not explain her arguments persuasively:
People have family commitments.

She uses rather dismissive language at the end:
As you wish.

3. Generally, Janek followed Katie's English very well, which indicates that she pitched it at the right level. However, there were two breakdowns due to the use of idiomatic expressions – *out of the blue* and *fed up* – neither of which Janek understands.

4. Involving a senior manager has both pros and cons. In terms of advantages, it offers access to experience and the authority which is sometimes needed to unblock major projects. On the downside, some senior managers expect operational managers in projects to solve problems on their own and not 'escalate' every interpersonal conflict which arises. If Katie has a solid relationship with her manager, it is a good idea to get a second perspective on an issue which can potentially damage a major project for her organisation.

5. One of the most important conflict management strategies in complex international contexts is recognition of conflict potential, early communication and commitment to joint problem solving. Katie should have recognised the risks early in the project and committed with AREMCO management to track the issue. Single training initiatives are seldom sufficient in such situations and a programme of ongoing induction into AREMCO's more complex systems would have been useful for Katie's staff. It might even have been an idea for AREMCO to transfer some of its staff to work with Katie's to coach and support with the reporting systems.

Phone calls, such as the example in this case, tend to happen when a lack of communication has allowed tensions to build and finally erupt. Regular, open and constructive communication is important to commit to and build into the culture of such projects right from the kick-off.

13

WRITING EMAIL: THE BASICS

Men of few words are the best men.

William Shakespeare, English poet and playwright (1564–1616)

Email is one of the most important tools of business communication in the world today. Surveys over the past ten years by the magazine *Business Spotlight* consistently show that email is the communication channel used most frequently by non-native speakers of English at work, and yet it is also one of the most badly used – by native and non-native speakers alike.

The unique nature of emailing can cause problems. The first problem is that it is fast and disposable, and so does not encourage careful communication. But the bigger problem is connected to user attitudes and behaviour.

In this chapter we look at some of the challenges of using email. We also propose solutions that take us back to the basic principles of communication presented in Chapters 2 and 3 of this book. And in the next chapter, we look at how to use email to carry out certain key management functions.

Before you read on, think about these questions:

1. What, for you, are the main differences between email and face-to-face communication?
2. How can you make sure that non-native speakers of English understand your emails?
3. How do you decide who to copy your emails to?
4. What is the best writing style for emails?

THE CHALLENGES

In the first chapter we outlined some basic principles of effective communication, using the sender-receiver model and T-I-P-S (Target, Information, Process, Style). We noted that:

- the sender's **T**arget must be right
- the **I**nformation must be clear
- the **P**rocess should be well defined, and that
- you should adapt your communication **S**tyle to get your message across to the receiver.

In this chapter we focus on *Process* because email is primarily a channel, not a style of communication. It is a form of interaction with unique features that can make communication more difficult than when it takes place face to face. Here are some of the main challenges of email.

Is this a good time?

In face-to-face communication we can normally judge whether to communicate now or whether to wait until a better moment. This is not the case with email. You cannot control the conditions in which an email is read. If the recipients of your emails open them when they are busy or in a bad mood, your communication can have a negative impact, although you may be unaware of this for some time.

Tip If you want to communicate sensitive information, it may be wiser to send an email to set up a telephone call to discuss the issue directly.

What do you think?

In face-to-face communication we can watch the recipients of our messages as we talk. We can assess their levels of understanding and agreement, and can modify our message accordingly. With email, we have to send the message in one block, and we are unable to clarify or qualify what we write until we receive a reply. Emails are therefore often seen as a little aggressive or 'pushy' and can feel much more one-way than face-to-face communication.

Tip There are a number of techniques using simple English that you can use to avoid seeming to be a little aggressive or 'pushy'.

- Start and end with basic courtesies: *Thanks for your email.*
- Encourage two-way communication by suggesting that your view may not be correct: *I may be wrong but I think we need a new approach. What do you think?*
- Show that you recognise that the other person is under pressure: *I appreciate that you are very busy …*
- Be open to renegotiating a deadline: *If it's a problem to get me the information by the end of this week, please let me know.*
- Express thanks for support when asking for information: *I'm very grateful for your support with this.*

A question of style

In face-to-face communication we not only adapt the content of our communication to the listener but also the way we say things. This is not possible when writing an email to someone for the first time.

Tip It is safest to adopt a neutral professional style. Aim to address people in a way that you think they will find respectful. You will be better able to assess the person's preferred style of email communication when they write back. Then you can adapt your own style accordingly.

What do you mean?

In face-to-face communication the person listening receives a message that is supported by non-verbal means of communication, such as body language or tone of voice. The reader of an email receives only the written words, making it more difficult to understand what is intended, particularly if the email has been written quickly and has been poorly constructed.

Tip Increase the clarity of your emails particularly for non-native speakers by using these techniques.

- Give the email a clear subject header, for example: *Meeting to discuss finances.*
- Avoid complex words and phrases.
- Organise key points into separate paragraphs that are either bulleted or numbered.
- Specify under each paragraph what the recipient has to do and by when.
- Inform the recipient why you need information by a certain date.
- Limit the number of different topics you deal with in a single email.

Who else needs to know?

In face-to-face communication the number of people you can communicate with is generally limited to how loudly you can shout – unless, of course, you are using a microphone with a large audience! With email there are no restrictions: it is possible to copy one email to thousands. A lot of people copy too many emails unnecessarily, which leads to email overload. On the other hand, you can cause resentment by not copying emails to those who feel they should be informed.

Tip Clarify expectations about copying emails, either directly with members of an international team, or via a mentor if you need advice on the policies and procedures in the organisation. Ask for feedback on a regular basis from recipients and non-recipients to check if you are getting it right. You can also get feedback on the style of your emails: too formal or informal? too much or too little information? too direct or indirect? and so on. You should always try to adapt your email style to your reader(s).

Did you get my email?

The speed of interaction in face-to-face communication is generally faster than with email. It may take a couple of days or even longer for the sender of an email to get a reply. If the receiver does not acknowledge an email, the sender is often left with the feeling that their message has disappeared into a black hole.

Tip Send short acknowledgements of emails when you think it is necessary (for example, because the subject matter is urgent) or when you think the other person would appreciate it.

What did you say?

In face-to-face communication, we exchange messages quickly but the words are forgotten almost as soon as they are spoken. Email is similarly fast for senders, but because the words are in writing, they may have a stronger impact, particularly if the message is critical. We also lose control of the text – our emails can be copied to others without our permission – so it is important to write carefully and respectfully at all times. Your reputation can be damaged if a 'blame mail' is copied to others, so think carefully before you click 'Send'. If in doubt, store the email and review it the next day.

Tip Do not write emails that might be perceived as aggressive and which would damage your reputation or cause problems for you if copied to others.

Look at the different ways below in which the same message can be constructed. The first version is very abrupt and potentially offensive.

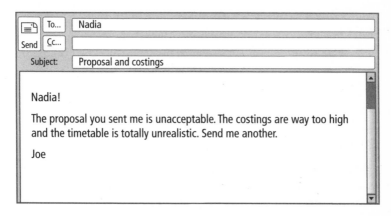

To... Nadia
Cc...
Subject: Proposal and costings

Nadia!

The proposal you sent me is unacceptable. The costings are way too high and the timetable is totally unrealistic. Send me another.

Joe

This second version is more professional and friendly.

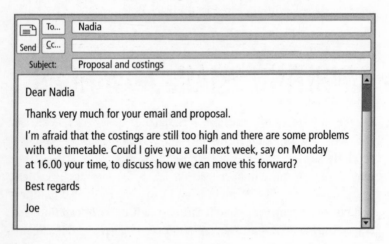

To... Nadia
Send Cc...
Subject: Proposal and costings

Dear Nadia

Thanks very much for your email and proposal.

I'm afraid that the costings are still too high and there are some problems with the timetable. Could I give you a call next week, say on Monday at 16.00 your time, to discuss how we can move this forward?

Best regards

Joe

A FINAL WORD

Emails are relatively easy to write and can quickly create the illusion of 'a job done'. However, poorly conceived and badly written emails waste everyone's time and cost organisations huge amounts of money in lost productivity.

So the next time you want to whizz off an email, try to compose a clear reason for writing, structure supporting information explicitly, and define a specific action or actions. Make it quick to read and easy to respond to. And look at the emails that come back to you. If you get what you asked for, your email was probably well written. If there is some form of misunderstanding, wrong data provided, clarification requested and so on, this could be feedback that your emails still offer some room for improvement.

14

WRITING EMAIL: ADVANCED

*What is written without effort
is in general read without pleasure.*

Samuel Johnson, English author and lexicographer (1709–84)

Section 2 of this book looked at core interpersonal skills such as building relationships, influencing people and resolving conflicts at work in the context of face-to-face communication. However, with the rise of virtual working, it is also important to understand how to do these things successfully when writing an email.

Before you read on, think about these questions:

1. How can you build business relationships by email?

2. How can you influence international business partners by email?

3. How can you manage conflict by email?

4. What are the dangers of using email for these communication tasks?

BUILDING RELATIONSHIPS

Success in business depends to an important extent on building positive relationships. Email may not seem at first to be the best medium for this task: text has a more impersonal character, and it is easy to misinterpret the written word without the support of body language and tone of voice. Indeed, email can often be a source of conflict rather than harmony at work. But if we use email carefully, and in the correct combination with other media, for example with telephone and face-to-face meetings, these criticisms need not apply.

So, how can email be used to build relationships? First, we need to remember that people have different approaches to relationship-building. Some want relationships to be close and informal. They want to be friends with their colleagues, laugh with them, share more personal information, and show interest in the lives of others. *Relationship-oriented* people like this might write an email like the one on page 171. As you read it, think about these two questions.

1. How would you feel if you received such an email?
2. How would you feel about writing such an email?

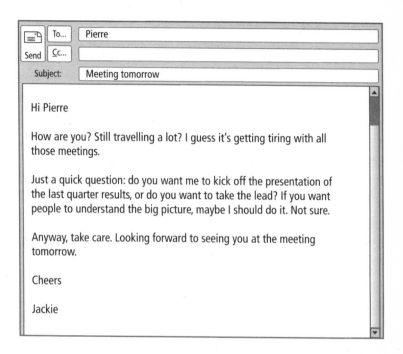

Task-oriented individuals, who often like to keep their personal and professional lives completely separate, and who often write more formally, might view this email as disrespectful and unprofessional. They might prefer to keep the tone neutral and concentrate purely on exchanging information.

The key message of this book is that communication is situational and has to be adapted to the specific person and to the specific context. If you tailor your email communication style and content to your readers, you can help to build professional respect in the same way as in face-to-face interactions.

The table on page 172 provides some tips on how you might use email to manage your relationships with two very different types of people: those who are relationship-oriented, and those who are task-oriented.

Managing relationships by email

Relationship	Relationship-oriented	Task-oriented
Style	Informal	Formal
	Light and humorous	Serious
	Begin with some personal details	Focus directly on business issues and needs
	Mention feelings	Stick to the facts
	Show interest in the other person	Keep emotions out of it
Frequency	Send frequent emails to keep in touch	Communicate only when you need to say something
	Blend email and telephone calls	Use email and avoid disturbing by phone

A TASK-ORIENTED EMAIL

How would you adapt Jackie's email if you had to deliver the same message to a more task-oriented individual? Compare your answer with the model in the Answer key at the end of the book.

INFLUENCING PEOPLE

The ability to influence others – for example, to build commitment to change or to persuade people to take on new responsibilities – is another key business skill. When you work internationally, with colleagues and customers across the world, much of this influencing has to be done by email.

As we saw in the last chapter, one of the problems with emails is that we cannot choose the conditions under which they are read. The recipient may simply be in the wrong mood to be influenced positively by what you write. Nevertheless, there are some general techniques that we can use to increase our ability to influence people by email.

BE STRUCTURED

One advantage of email is that we have the time to organise and present information logically, and to provide all the relevant detail to support an argument. In face-to-face communication, listeners can interrupt or sidetrack a speaker. Another advantage of the written word is that the message is documented clearly. This can help as a reference point during complex negotiations or difficult discussions. Here is an example of a clearly structured email.

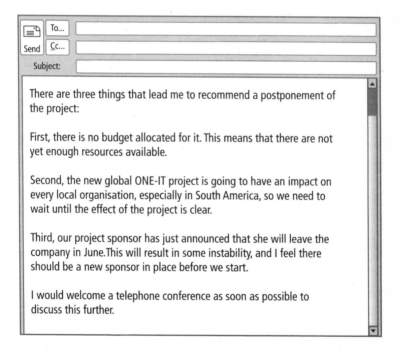

There are three things that lead me to recommend a postponement of the project:

First, there is no budget allocated for it. This means that there are not yet enough resources available.

Second, the new global ONE-IT project is going to have an impact on every local organisation, especially in South America, so we need to wait until the effect of the project is clear.

Third, our project sponsor has just announced that she will leave the company in June. This will result in some instability, and I feel there should be a new sponsor in place before we start.

I would welcome a telephone conference as soon as possible to discuss this further.

BE INTERACTIVE

Because you cannot support your email with a smile or quick clarification, it is easy for the recipient to misinterpret your motives. Use the three-step 'multimedia sandwich' to get around this problem.

Step 1

Use the telephone or a face-to-face meeting (or both) before you try to influence people in writing. Ask questions to find out their basic opinions, their key resistance points and their openness to persuasion.

Step 2

Write the email with clear arguments, and finish with a request to follow up with a telephone call or a face-to-face meeting. You may also state your willingness to consider other ideas to show openness.

Step 3

Call or meet the person(s) concerned to present your arguments, hear their responses and deal with any resistance points.

USE HIERARCHY

Another way to influence people by using email is to copy in a more senior manager. The aim here is to increase the pressure on a recipient to take your email seriously and comply with your request. However, such escalation may well be seen as an unacceptable threat, and can create negative feelings and damage a relationship, so you need to think very carefully about the different possible outcomes if you decide on this approach.

MANAGING CONFLICT

Let us now look at an example of conflict management via email. The email on page 175 is from Bill Benson to Carole Schlautmann. Carole is an international project manager to whom one of Bill's line staff, Jacques Sampers, has to report as a member of her project team. Bill expresses his worries about Jacques's role in the project.

As you read the email:

1. think about how you would feel in Carole's position
2. underline any parts of the email that you find problematic
3. think of ways that you could improve the text.

Bill's email could be viewed quite negatively. It seems to have an accusing tone (... *pressure you are putting him under*), and Bill seems

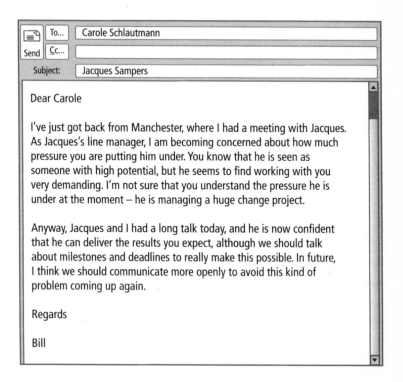

To... Carole Schlautmann

Cc...

Subject: Jacques Sampers

Dear Carole

I've just got back from Manchester, where I had a meeting with Jacques. As Jacques's line manager, I am becoming concerned about how much pressure you are putting him under. You know that he is seen as someone with high potential, but he seems to find working with you very demanding. I'm not sure that you understand the pressure he is under at the moment – he is managing a huge change project.

Anyway, Jacques and I had a long talk today, and he is now confident that he can deliver the results you expect, although we should talk about milestones and deadlines to really make this possible. In future, I think we should communicate more openly to avoid this kind of problem coming up again.

Regards

Bill

to be saying that Carole has failed to build an effective relationship with Jacques (*I'm not sure that you understand the pressure he is under* ...). In fact, it is quite easy to identify a few techniques that Bill could use to soften his message. Here are some of the things that one might recommend.

Mix criticism in with praise ('positive framing')

Bill could have written: *Jacques really enjoys working with you and finds the project very interesting, but I am concerned about how much pressure you are putting him under.*

Be explicit about what you are not saying to reduce the risk of negative interpretation

Bill could have written: *I am not criticising you in any way, Carole, but I am very concerned about how much pressure Jacques is under.*

Make clear you are expressing a view, not stating facts

Bill could have written: *In my opinion, it would be a good idea to talk about milestones and deadlines …*

These all look like good techniques, and it might indeed be a good idea for Bill to adopt them. But the most important point is not what Bill writes but how the reader – in this case Carole – interprets his message. Conflict is initiated less by other people's behaviour than by how we read that behaviour, and how quickly we make negative judgements. In fact, there are many positive aspects to Bill's email. How many of these did you see?

Positive intent

Bill discusses a problem proactively. Perhaps he is motivated by openness and honesty.

Results-orientated

Bill clearly wants to get results both internationally and in his local office.

People-focused

Bill is protecting Jacques. This may be from a sense of organisational responsibility (Jacques has a talent that needs to be nurtured), but it may also be motivated by another positive quality – loyalty.

Closed dialogue

The email stays private. There is no escalation of the issue through the involvement of another party. So discretion seems to be another of Bill's positive qualities.

Diplomacy

Bill's email is quite diplomatic. Nothing in it necessarily communicates any sense of blame or personal attack. He keeps to the facts and invites further dialogue to resolve differences of opinion.

In fact, there is not a single sentence in Bill's email that we cannot interpret as having a positive intention. So, in finding fault with this email and suggesting improvements, we may be guilty of making unfair assumptions about Bill's motives. In other words, we may be the real generators of conflict by email.

This leads us to three tips for reading emails.

1. Do not react too quickly

When you judge something negatively, you are probably imposing your own values on the situation. Remember this when you feel negative emotions appearing. Start the habit of rereading the emails you receive.

2. Read positive intention

Look for any positives, even in emails that seem to attack you (or others). This allows you to respond more positively. There will nearly always be positives if you are open enough to spot them.

3. Think beyond the person and think about processes

Emails that discuss problems may be a sign of organisational difficulties. (Jacques is involved in two projects, which may mean that the company lacks resources.) Look at the possible systemic issues behind a conflict and try not to see everything as a clash of personalities.

DEVELOPING YOUR EMAIL SKILLS

Take a look at some of the emails that you have written recently and see how effectively you built relationships, influenced people and managed conflict. Then try to integrate some of the ideas from this chapter into your future emails. Also, monitor the emails that you receive as a way of assessing the success of your communication. If you continue this process over a period of time, you should find yourself writing more sensitively and effectively – and achieving better business results.

15

TELEPHONING

Connecting people

Advertising slogan of Nokia,
Finnish multinational communications corporation

In every modern office you see people sitting at their desks or standing in corridors with their mobile phones. But what are they doing? Quite often they are not talking but rather reading their emails and sending text messages. The telephone is being used more and more now for exchanging text. This is a pity because speaking over the phone to someone has many advantages over written communication.

In this chapter we make the case for a more intensive and targeted use of the telephone, with tips on specific language and communication strategies. Before you read on, think about these questions:

1. Why do people, especially non-native speakers, often prefer to send an email rather than phone?
2. What is the best way to start a call?
3. What makes a good voicemail message?
4. What is the right way to deal with customer complaints?

PHONE OR EMAIL?

There are a number of good reasons why people prefer to send an email rather than use the phone.

1. Telephone calls often have to be scheduled, which can be complicated. It can seem simpler to send an email and let people reply in their own time. Indeed, this makes sense when you are just asking for information as people may need time to find the information you want.

2. Speaking on the phone is much more challenging for many non-native speakers than the relative safety of email. This is particularly true if the person on the other end of the phone has a strong accent or speaks very fast or unclearly (or all three!).

3. Email allows you to document what you are saying and therefore keep other people informed. This can be very important when there is conflict or disagreement. What was said and promised during a telephone call can be disputed but the contents of an email are there for anyone to see.

So, what are the three big advantages of picking up your phone and calling someone?

1 It is personal

Talking to people on the phone generally offers better opportunities for relationship building than email. You hear their voices and you have at least a chance of reading their feelings. You can spend time listening to their problems. You can convince others that you take an interest in them in a way that is not so easy by email. And because a call is (probably) not being recorded, you can be more open with your own feelings than you might be in an email.

2 It is immediate

Communication should be more efficient on the telephone. We can clarify as we speak. We can put things another way if people do not understand us the first time. We can check whether people understand with quick follow-up questions. In theory, we can do all of this by email, but it sometimes take days to reach an understanding by email while we can reach the same understanding in a telephone call in minutes.

3 It offers added value

Emails tend to be more focused than telephone calls. When we talk on the phone, we can discuss other topics, gossip, and catch up on other subjects that may have an impact on our work.

Think about your main communication channels at work. How much time do you give to each? Should you be allocating your time differently?

MANAGING THE MEDIUM

Talking on the phone is very similar to talking face to face. But there are some features of the telephone that mean we have to use specific communication and language strategies.

1 GETTING CONNECTED

The first challenge is the basic one of getting connected to the right person. This may not seem to be an issue in the age of mobile phones. Surely you can simply dial the number and the right person will answer. Unfortunately, it is not always that easy and there are two scenarios which can prove problematic.

You have to connect via another person

Imagine that you have to make a call to a new contact, and have to go via a third person – a personal assistant or the company switchboard. If the third person's English skills are not strong, and the pronunciation of your name – or that of the person you wish to speak to – is problematic, getting connected may be challenging. Minimise any difficulties by making sure you:

- can pronounce the name of your contact clearly and accurately
- know the title and department of the person, to help the switchboard understand who you want to talk to

- can say and spell your name slowly and clearly. Be tolerant if the person makes mistakes.

Personal assistants act as gatekeepers for their managers. If you are ringing with a scheduled appointment, you will probably be put through quite quickly. If you are calling without an appointment, you may have to sell the necessity for the call.

You have to leave a message

It is important when leaving a message to be concise (try to keep the message below 30 seconds), to be clear about how urgent the issue is, and to suggest what should happen next (who calls whom, on which number, and when).

2 STARTING UP

The style of introduction – whether you are making or answering a call – depends on a number of factors.

Cultural context and individual preferences

Some people use only their family name to identify themselves when they pick up the phone. Others may use a formula designed by their organisation to promote an image of good customer service.

The relationship between the people

Callers introduce themselves to another person in a style that characterises their professional relationship, either formal or less formal. With caller ID display, the person calling may not need – or have the opportunity – to make an introduction. The receiver often knows who is calling and can greet the caller immediately.

Checking if someone is free to talk

With an unscheduled call, and even sometimes with scheduled calls, it is important to check if the person is available and free to talk.

Rescheduling

Calls frequently have to be rescheduled due to unforeseen events or office pressures. Be prepared for this and do not judge it as a sign of inefficiency in your counterpart.

Small talk or down to business?

We have the same dilemma on the phone as when meeting face to face: how much time should we invest in small talk and when should we get down to business? Choose a style that is appropriate for the person you are talking to and the context. If there is an emergency, you will obviously not spend hours discussing the weather. However, it may be helpful with international contacts to first ask a few polite questions to create a positive atmosphere for the discussion. But keep this short and simple: remember that non-native speakers can find small talk challenging because they do not have a large general vocabulary.

Agreeing the purpose of the call

As with face-to-face meetings, it is important to clarify the purpose and process of the phone call. If the call has been scheduled and an agenda set in an email, this can be referred to and agreed in very much the same way as in a meeting.

3 DURING THE CALL

Telephone communication is more challenging because we do not usually have the visual supports that help us to assess what someone is really saying, how strongly they feel, how far they agree with an idea, etc. This makes it important to activate many of the communication principles outlined in the first two chapters of this book.

Keep It Short and Simple (KISS)

When speaking on the phone, keep your messages short. Also, make clear the reasons for your message so that people can understand why you are saying what you are saying.

Check

When listening, we need to clarify a lot in order to check our understanding.

Move on

If we rely simply on someone's voice, it can be difficult to hear when it is time to move to the next topic or whether people want to keep talking about the current issue. This needs to be explicitly clarified.

4 CLOSING THE CALL

As with face-to-face communication, it is important to handle well the transition from discussion to the end of the conversation. For example, you can use a simple phrase like *So, is there anything else?* But be aware that these linguistic signals for moving from one topic to the next or closing a call may differ across cultures. Your signals may not be so obvious to your counterpart, and vice versa. Also, take the time to summarise the call and to list any actions that have been agreed.

Very often people end calls too quickly because they want to end the stressful experience! But after summarising, use the opportunities that a telephone contact can offer, particularly with colleagues who are overseas.

- Find out about other relevant issues.
- Ask about what is going on in the local organisation.
- Look for opportunities to expand your network.

COMPLAINTS AND CUSTOMER SERVICE

One of the most challenging telephone situations is dealing with an angry customer who wants to make a complaint. Here are some basic guidelines.

The buck stops here

Accept personal responsibility because, for the customer, you *are* your company or organisation.

Admit the mistake

Do not try to defend yourself or your organisation, even if you think you are right. If the customer feels something has gone wrong, then it has! There are two key rules for dealing with customers. Rule one: the customer is always right. Rule two: if the customer is wrong, see rule one!

Apologise and empathise

Make sure that the customer knows you understand the inconvenience caused, and that you sympathise with him/her. Do not be afraid to apologise. That does not mean that you are admitting to some personal mistake. Practise saying sorry.

Act now

Do what you can immediately to start the process of putting things right. If it is impossible to deal with the problem straightaway, get agreement on a clear time frame.

Offer compensation

Some small compensation is often enough to satisfy a customer. It shows that you value the business they are bringing to you and that you are interested in a long-term relationship.

Thank the customer

Surveys show that for every customer who complains, there are more than twenty 'silent sufferers'. So you should be grateful for the feedback that this one is giving you, even if it is expressed negatively.

PICK UP THE PHONE

Modern business culture has become too dependent on email and text as means of communication, despite all their advantages. It is time to pick up the phone and start talking to people again. This needs careful time management. It also means developing more confidence with your English, and thinking carefully about the appropriate communication strategies. But the telephone can offer real benefits in professional communication and, if used properly, can create strong foundations for trust and effective cooperation.

16

TAKING PART IN CONFERENCE CALLS

'Researchers find that attendees of business videoconferences must work harder to interpret information delivered during a conference call than they would if they attended face-to-face meetings.

Wikipedia, web-based, collaborative encyclopedia, launched 2001

Telephone and video conferences are now a key part of international business life, especially for people working in international teams.

In this chapter we focus mainly on the challenge of telephone conference calls or virtual meetings, and suggest ways to make them work better. We will also give you tips on how to handle the specific challenges of virtual meetings when using video conferencing technology.

Before you read on, think about these questions:

1. What can you do to prepare effectively for international conference calls?
2. What is the best way to start a conference call?
3. What techniques can help you lead virtual meetings effectively?
4. What is good etiquette for participants in virtual meetings?

PREPARING

To be successful, conference calls need effective planning. The first step is to decide on the right mix of virtual and face-to-face meetings for the people involved. For example, face-to-face meetings every few months may be necessary to maintain trust and to help with effective information exchange in the conference calls.

The second step concerns the purpose of conference calls, deciding what can be achieved in a virtual environment. Difficult decisions or conflicts are probably best dealt with offline, on a one-to-one or one-to-two basis, and then reported back to the larger group. Conference calls involving larger numbers of people are best suited to updating, briefing, and relatively simple decisions about goals and actions.

Getting the logistics right is critical to the success of conference calls.

PEOPLE

It may be helpful to talk to people individually before the call to discuss the objectives and desired outcomes. Of course, this is also helpful for face-to-face meetings, but it is even more important for conference calls as there is less opportunity for clarification of viewpoints during the event.

ORGANISATION

- When announcing the conference call via email, make sure the timing is clear to everyone, particularly when people are in different time zones.
- If the meeting is longer than 90 minutes, plan breaks to keep people fresh and inform people of these in advance.

TECHNOLOGY

- Make sure that you are familiar with the conference call environment and technology.

- Check that all necessary login and passwords have been sent and received.
- Log in to the conference call five or ten minutes before the official start time to check that everything is working.
- Advise people on potential quality problems in advance. Be aware that some telephone conferencing systems lose quality when people dial in using a mobile or cordless phone.
- Have a back-up plan in case of serious technical problems. For example, have alternative dial in/log in numbers in case of connection problems.

INFORMATION

- Create an agenda that is clear about the outcomes, process, timing and roles.
- Send participants the agenda and supporting documents well in advance and tell them which documents will be used or referred to at which point in the meeting.
- Translate important documents for people whose English may not be good.
- Number all documents so that it is easy to refer to them during the call.

GETTING STARTED

The person leading or facilitating the meeting should enter the virtual environment first and be ready to welcome the others as they arrive. Most telephone conference calls indicate if you are first into the conference. If this is not indicated, you know that other people are already present.

As people log in, the chair can initiate small talk or informal introductions between participants, if numbers allow for this: with a large number of participants it may be difficult. Participants should make sure that their arrival is noted by the chair and then say a few words of introduction. These opening moments can be chaotic, particularly at the start of telephone conference calls, so saying less rather than more can help the chair to keep control.

TIPS FOR SUCCESSFUL CHAIRING

- Set the right tone for the meeting with positive comments to participants.
- Introduce early arrivals to later arrivals as a team-building activity.
- Do formal introductions of new members.
- For telephone conference calls, a roll call (checking that people are present person by person) is useful to make clear who is at the meeting.
- Check and then deal with technical problems.
- Find out if anyone has to leave early so you know whether the order of the points on the agenda will work or not.
- Ensure that the objectives of the meeting are clear.
- Review and amend the agenda as necessary.
- Clarify any rules at the start to ensure an efficient process (see the box below).
- Start the discussion and then invite people by name to take part. Start with people who are likely to show a positive attitude.

'RULES' FOR VIRTUAL MEETING COMMUNICATION

As with face-to-face meetings, defining rules will help an international group to interact more successfully. Here are some suggestions.

1. Announce names before giving an opinion – particularly important in telephone conference calls.
2. Indicate to whom a question is addressed.
3. Give everyone the chance to speak.
4. Accept the chairperson's authority to interrupt.
5. Speak slowly and clearly.

MANAGING THE DISCUSSION

The choice of approach for conference calls depends very much on the number of participants and the objectives. Typically, the more participants there are present, and the more it is a briefing event, the more directive the chairing style has to be. In smaller groups, a more facilitating style which encourages interaction may be appropriate. Of course, both styles may be adopted by the chairperson during the same meeting at different times.

THE DIRECTIVE STYLE

When chairpersons use a directive style, they tend to:

- narrow the scope of the discussion to save time
- use closed questions to produce short answers (*Does everyone agree?*)
- discourage discussion between participants
- push hard towards decisions by suggesting solutions
- interrupt speakers who talk for a long time.

If you decide to use a more directive style in a virtual meeting, it can be helpful to explain why. Otherwise, some participants may react against what they see as a too authoritarian approach.

THE EMPOWERING STYLE

When chairpersons use an empowering style, they tend to:

- encourage discussion and avoid pushing their own agenda
- stimulate creative thinking by asking lots of open questions (*What does everyone think about this?*)
- ask participants to comment on each others' ideas to reach a group solution
- allow time for people to speak, but interrupt those who speak too much.

THE VALUE OF SUMMARISING

Whichever style you adopt, remember that conference calls, particularly telephone-only conferences, place far heavier demands on non-native speakers than face-to-face communication does. So the chairperson must clarify and summarise frequently to make sure that everyone understands what has been said. When running a web-based conference with the option to share documents and applications, it can also be a good idea to write the minutes during the meeting. This makes the results of the discussion transparent to all as the meeting progresses and helps people to clarify or disagree with points more easily.

ENCOURAGING PARTICIPATION

Chairpersons in conference calls often have to work extra hard to get everyone to say anything. Here are a number of techniques that can help.

- Use people's names frequently to keep their attention, particularly during telephone conferences.
- Go round the group occasionally to check the opinions of all participants or use on-screen polling features in web-based applications.
- Offer breaks so that people can stretch their legs and think about what they want to say.
- Encourage people to use an interactive whiteboard or text box in web conferencing software to post comments for discussion.

THE ROLE OF THE PARTICIPANT: LISTENING

Listening as a participant during conference calls can be more challenging than in face-to-face meetings. Sound quality can be poor, and visual information is absent in telephone conference calls and reduced in video-based ones. Participants should decide whether to adopt a more proactive or a more reactive listening style, depending on the context of each call.

PROACTIVE LISTENING

Proactive listeners use a number of techniques to support communication in virtual meetings. They tend to:

- make acknowledging noises (such as *uh-huh, OK, yes, …*) to indicate understanding and/or agreement
- reformulate the comments of other people to check understanding
- ask follow-up questions to get more information
- send positive signals to people, even when disagreeing with what they are saying
- suggest ways of discussing the issue more efficiently.

REACTIVE LISTENING

Reactive listeners are more passive. They generally:

- remain silent (thinking: *I don't want to disturb the speaker.*)
- do not spend time summarising other people's ideas (thinking: *If it's understood, why waste time?*)
- do not intervene when the meeting goes off track (thinking: *This is the chair's responsibility.*)
- do not give much positive feedback during the meeting (thinking: *I can give the feedback in a personal call or email later.*)
- do not interrupt (thinking: *I don't want to be impolite.*)

The listening style or combination of styles which you choose will depend a lot on the number of participants and the hierarchical relationships between them. Large numbers and strong hierarchies can make it difficult to use proactive listening strategies, as this may be seen as time-wasting, disruptive and even disrespectful. On the other hand, overusing the reactive style is dangerous because it places all the responsibility for directing and clarifying in the hands of the chair, who may struggle as a non-native speaker of English.

PARTICIPANT ETIQUETTE

- Inform the meeting leader by text or email if you are going to be significantly late.
- Connect from a quiet location and use the mute button when not speaking to avoid background noise.
- If possible, avoid mobile and cordless phones as they can reduce the quality of the connection.
- Do not multi-task if your participation is important: remove other papers from your desk and give the meeting your full attention.

THE ROLE OF THE PARTICIPANT: SPEAKING

Many of the principles of speaking presented in Chapter 2 apply to conference calls. Here are some specific tips to support speaking in virtual meetings.

- Make your voice interesting to listen to by using a positive tone, varied intonation, the right volume and moderate tempo.

- Remember that it is more difficult to understand complex input in a virtual environment, particularly in telephone conference calls. Make your input more understandable by simplifying wherever possible, structuring the message clearly, and making use of supporting documents with clear references to page numbers.
- Avoid the 'one-way effect' where people listen in silence for long periods. Show your understanding of the views of others and express openness to interruptions so that you create a sense of dialogue.
- Use a clear handover to signal to others that you have stopped speaking and that others may now comment or add opinions.

SORRY TO INTERRUPT BUT ...

Getting the opportunity to speak can be difficult in conference calls, especially with large numbers of participants. Many non-native speakers lack the confidence and sense of timing to interrupt politely. Some see interruption as impolite in principle and remain silent as a sign of respect. Others find it difficult to know when someone is going to stop speaking and whether others also want to interrupt. The result can be domination by the more assertive communicators, often the native speakers.

It is important, therefore, to practise some simple phrases to interrupt, such as *Sorry to interrupt but ...* or *I agree with that, and I'd like to add that* .... It is probably best to avoid using the expression *Yes, but ...*, as this may sound negative.

CLOSING

Allow more time than in face-to-face meetings for explicit summarising and checking. Participants with lower levels of English competence in particular will welcome the opportunity to go over decisions again.

If you are leading a virtual meeting, you should follow up with a personal telephone call to anyone who you think may not have understood the decisions or who is not fully committed to them. This form of post-meeting management is essential for virtual meetings because it is easier for participants to hide their disagreement and lack of commitment by simply saying nothing.

IMPROVE YOUR CONFERENCE CALLS

Take a few minutes at the end to do after-call feedback. The chair can either request feedback directly or can send an email request after the meeting. This creates opportunities to clarify issues and also produces a more open conference-call culture. Alternatively, you could use a more formal feedback sheet similar to the one below.

CONFERENCE CALL FEEDBACK SHEET

Score your answer to each question on a scale of 1–5 (1 = completely unacceptable, 2 = unsatisfactory, 3 = satisfactory, 4 = good, 5 = excellent).

1. How well was the conference call facilitated?
   How could facilitation be improved?

2. How good was the technology?
   How could we improve the way we use it?

3. How effective was the interaction between participants?
   How could we improve it?

4. How well did you understand the discussion?
   How could we improve understanding?

5. What other ideas do you have to improve our conference calls?

PREPARE FOR THE FUTURE

Virtual working is increasing and will probably be the commonest form of interaction between professionals working in global teams for large international organisations in the future. The skills you need to lead and interact in virtual meeting environments – both audio and video – are evolving all the time. It is therefore important that you have a plan to improve your virtual communication skills to meet this new challenge.

17

WORKING IN VIRTUAL TEAMS

Out of sight, out of mind.

Thomas à Kempis, German Catholic monk and writer (1380–1471)

As discussed in earlier chapters, professional people are finding themselves working more and more in global virtual teams. Team members in different locations rely more and more on electronic channels of communication such as video and audio conferencing (see Chapter 16). Virtual teams may also use professional and social networking technologies such as Wikis or team Facebook sites to distribute and share information.

Virtual team workers regularly report that communication is a challenge and that relationships are difficult to build and maintain. Gone are those all important catch-up opportunities around the coffee machine, or the unplanned but invaluable meetings in the corridors as people rush between meetings. People struggle to find the right moment to connect, partly due also to the pressures of working within different time zones. And when people do hook up, technological and cultural barriers present further hurdles to common understanding.

In this final chapter we summarise the major challenges of working in a virtual team and give you the opportunity to rate your skills. Before you read on, think about these three questions:

1. How can you build trust in a global virtual team?
2. When should virtual team members communicate electronically and when is it necessary to communicate face to face?

3. Which communication skills are particularly important for members of virtual teams?

4. What can members of virtual teams do to manage their time effectively when working under a lot of pressure?

WHAT PEOPLE SAY ABOUT VIRTUAL TEAMS

Despite the everyday challenges of working in a team whose members are all at the same location, it seems that people generally prefer face-to-face teams to virtual ones. Look at these typical comments made by professionals about their experience of working virtually. Which statements do you agree with most and are closest to your views? Why?

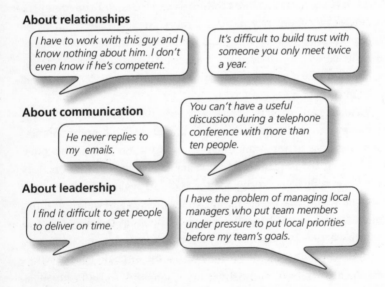

About relationships

> I have to work with this guy and I know nothing about him. I don't even know if he's competent.

> It's difficult to build trust with someone you only meet twice a year.

About communication

> He never replies to my emails.

> You can't have a useful discussion during a telephone conference with more than ten people.

About leadership

> I find it difficult to get people to deliver on time.

> I have the problem of managing local managers who put team members under pressure to put local priorities before my team's goals.

THE GOOD VIRTUAL WORKER

What characteristics do you need to be an effective virtual worker? In this section, we provide some suggestions and give you the opportunity to rate your skills.

GOOD TECHNICAL SKILLS

It is important for virtual team members to be familiar with all types of technology, including video and audio conferencing platforms, group database systems, and new software and networking technologies that can be used to plan and record team work. Particularly useful is the ability to troubleshoot and solve the irritating glitches that can arise during conference calls.

But virtual team workers should not be over-technical. It is also important to know when to use which technology, and when not to use technology at all and instead set up a face-to-face meeting. This can be particularly important for discussions of sensitive or complex issues.

> **RATE YOUR TECHNOLOGY COMPETENCE**
> (high) 5 - 4 - 3 - 2 - 1 (low)
>
> I feel comfortable with technology.   ○
>
> I can solve minor technical problems.   ○
>
> I can match the right technology to the right job.   ○
>
> I know when not to use technology.   ○

THE ABILITY TO WORK INDEPENDENTLY

Being a member of a virtual team means working without regular supervision. A higher level manager is no longer walking past your desk every day to check on what you are doing. So effective virtual workers need to be independent, motivated self-starters who can work hard and deliver high quality without being given lots of instructions. They need the tolerance to accept that changing project targets may mean that they have to throw away what they have done and start again. They also need to be able to take leadership responsibilities and to be proactive in foreseeing and solving problems.

RATE YOUR LEVEL OF INDEPENDENCE
(high) 5 - 4 - 3 - 2 - 1 (low)

I feel comfortable working without supervision.   ◯

I am motivated to deliver high quality on my own.   ◯

I am tolerant of working with changing targets.   ◯

I am proactive in identifying and solving problems.   ◯

GOOD TIME MANAGEMENT SKILLS

Virtual workers need to be excellent time managers who can prioritise local and virtual team tasks effectively and meet their deadlines. They should communicate their work status regularly to relevant managers, and reply promptly to emails to avoid senders wondering when their urgent email is going to be answered. Time management also means setting time aside for other things in life: to take training courses, to bring relevant new skills into the team, to have a life outside work, to reflect and to relax.

RATE YOUR TIME MANAGEMENT COMPETENCE
(high) 5 - 4 - 3 - 2 - 1 (low)

I prioritise local and virtual team tasks effectively.   ◯

I communicate work status regularly.   ◯

I respond promptly to emails.   ◯

I make time to relax and for life outside work.   ◯

GOOD TEAM SKILLS

Although virtual team members need to be strongly independent, they must also know when to support and cooperate with others in the team in order to reach common goals. They should show explicitly that they are ready to help others and to share information.

This helps to create a supportive environment and encourages the development of trust.

Good virtual team workers also make efforts to learn about the other members of their team, to appreciate the challenges of their working environments, and to get to know their areas of competence and possible weaknesses. This requires a lot of communication (for example via email and telephone calls), taking the time to ask questions and listen to others. The time that is invested in this relationship building may seem to offer little value in the short term, but it will enable the team to perform more effectively in the longer term.

Finally, as team players, effective virtual workers try to make life easier for others. They avoid causing extra work, and volunteer to take on additional tasks themselves. Above all, they do not blame or criticise other team members when things go wrong. They appreciate that different working styles are good for teamwork, and seek to exploit the advantages of diversity as much as possible.

RATE YOUR TEAM PLAYER SKILLS
(high) 5 - 4 - 3 - 2 - 1 (low)

I like to help others and share information. ◯

I try to learn about others and their contexts. ◯

I make time for relationship building. ◯

I have a positive attitude to diversity in the team. ◯

GOOD COMMUNICATION SKILLS

Above all, effective virtual workers are good communicators. They give the right information at the right level of detail at the right time. Too much or too little information can create stress and confusion. This does not mean that 'Keeping It Short and Simple' (KISS) is always the right approach. Sometimes it can be important to say more than usual, to make explicit your assumptions and intentions. This enables others to understand you better and respond appropriately.

Those leading virtual meetings need to communicate extensively both before the meeting (to assess attitudes and levels of engagement) as well as after the meeting (to assess levels of understanding and commitment to the decisions taken, and to get feedback). Not doing this with key participants poses a real risk to the effectiveness of team decision-making.

Finally, remember that distance reduces the opportunities for informal communication, and for saying what is going well in the team and what needs to be improved. When leading a virtual team, it is important to create a range of opportunities for people to give and get feedback on the team's performance, from one-to-one calls, to brainstorming team improvements together.

RATE YOUR COMMUNICATION SKILLS
(high) 5 - 4 - 3 - 2 - 1 (low)

I give information at the right level at the right time. ◯

I state explicitly my assumptions and intentions. ◯

I discuss agendas before, and decisions after meetings. ◯

I create a range of opportunities to give and get feedback. ◯

AND FINALLY …

Working effectively in a virtual team, and helping the team to work as a team, needs commitment from everyone involved. All too often, people do not show that commitment because of work pressure or lack of direct supervision. As a result, their virtual teams become less efficient.

We believe that following the ideas in this final chapter, and discussing these ideas within your teams, offers you a greater chance of success when communicating internationally.

CASE STUDY 4

'CAN I SAY SOMETHING,
PLEASE?'

CASE STUDY 4

Read the case study which illustrates some of the challenges which occur when communicating internationally. Then answer the questions and compare your answers with the case commentary.

◇◇◇

'Can I say something, please?'

Caroline Deschamps was responsible for global product innovation in the confectionery division of one of the world's leading multinational food companies. An important part of her job was to facilitate creative information exchange meetings (CIE meetings) between heads of product development in a number of key countries. These exchanges were normally conducted within a monthly telephone conference call which lasted for three hours. Caroline found these meetings very challenging to facilitate. Some individuals dominated the discussion whilst others were extremely quiet. She realised that it was causing frustration for some individuals in the meeting as she occasionally received emails like this one.

Dear Caroline

Many thanks for to organise the call conference yesterday. Again, however, I must say I feel a little angry. Three members, all native English speakers, talked all time and trying to dominate, especially Bob. The decisions we have made reflect this. I do not agree the current structure of our meetings helps non-native speakers to give their ideas. Native speakers are dominating with their language advantage. I am not sure how we deal with the problem. Is possible we discuss by phone next week?

Regards

Juan

Caroline decided to forward the email in confidence to the most talkative of the native English speakers to inform him of the problem which has been reported. She received the following email in reply.

Caroline

I'm really unhappy about the email which you forwarded. I contribute enthusiastically and openly in all of our meetings, and I do not expect to be told that I am 'trying to dominate'. As far as I'm concerned, the problem is nothing to do with language. We are part of a bigger business unit with more experience of this kind of innovation. So we simply have more to say. Our markets are more important for the company, so it's natural that the decisions reflect these priorities. The smaller countries are, well, smaller countries.

To be honest, I think if people have something to contribute, they should say something in the meetings rather than write emails. It is their responsibility to speak up. I'm happy to be guided more by you as a facilitator in the meetings but if I have ideas to contribute, then I have a professional obligation to express them.

Best

Bob

Caroline realised that she had to clarify the situation with the team, and decided to add *Improving conference call communication* to the agenda of the next team meeting.

QUESTIONS

1. How far do you think that native English speakers were causing a problem in the conference calls?

2. What do you think of Caroline's decision to forward Juan's email to Bob?

3. What do you feel about the style and content of Bob's email to Caroline?

4. What do you think of Caroline's idea to discuss the topic at the next team meeting?

OVER TO YOU

Communicating virtually via telephone conference calls has become a core component of international business. Yet almost everyone experiences these calls or meetings as problematic in some way. Non-native English speakers regularly complain about the domination of native speakers in such calls.

1. What are the main challenges that you experience when communicating virtually in conference calls or via email?

2. How do you modify your own behaviour as a native speaker during conference calls to make your contribution as effective as possible for everyone?

COMMENTARY

1. Without listening to actual recordings of the conference calls, it is difficult with certainty to ascribe blame to the English native speakers as Juan did. However, Juan's perception is very real and the native English speakers probably bear a significant responsibility for this, since it is quite possible that they are speaking too fast, for too long and are using over-complex English. It is also probable that the native English speakers were unaware that the language they were using is causing a problem; they may even believe they had slowed down their delivery enough. It is unlikely that they were consciously exploiting their language advantage to influence decisions.

2. We should not forward confidential emails (whether explicitly or implicitly identified as such) to other people. Doing so risks damaging the trust of the writer of the original email. However, Juan's situation highlights the fact that we have little control over emails after they have been sent: once forwarded, they may be read out of context and this may generate serious misunderstanding. Telephone calls or face-to-face conversation are better channels to communicate such sensitive information.

3. It is easy to see Bob's email as defensive in tone and not very constructive. However, he introduced some very valid points, namely that the dynamic of international meeting communication is often influenced by disparate levels of experience, and relative business unit power and interests. Moreover, Bob pointed out that the failings of communication fall on all parties including the non-native English speakers for not asserting themselves, interrupting the native speakers and/or using alternative strategies to get their point of view heard in meetings, for example by discussing on a one-to-one basis with the meeting leader prior to the actual event. He was also constructive in suggesting that he is open to be guided more by the meeting facilitator, an excellent invitation to Caroline to show more leadership.

   However, Bob seems not to appreciate the levels of frustration shown by Juan, and his own role in creating this feeling. This may indicate a lack of self-awareness and a general lack of sensitivity to issues of international communication.

4. Open discussion in a team meeting of such an issue can productively lead to common understanding and a joint commitment to communicate more collaboratively. It can also lead to defensiveness, blaming of 'the other', and dangerous levels of conflict. Caroline should have networked with individuals in advance of the meeting to assess levels of feeling and ideas on how to solve the problem before committing to an open discussion during a conference call which is not suited to debating complex issues.

CONCLUSION

The important thing is to not stop questioning.

Albert Einstein, theoretical physicist (1879–1955)

It is difficult to draw simple conclusions from what is a very complex subject. However, one message which comes from experienced international communicators is surprisingly simple: just ask more questions, particularly those which clarify what others are telling you, and which check whether others have understood your message.

And there is a clear reason for this simple advice. If we have the courage to ask more questions, we get two very important benefits.

1. We are seen as more open by our international partners, which helps us build better relationships.
2. We learn things that we did not expect to learn. We get better quality information. This better information helps us to achieve better results.

Successful international communicators are often very curious people. They like to ask lots of questions to understand others, to understand the cultures in which they work, to comprehend the complex forces at play in the business landscape. This helps them to take the right decisions. But knowledge is never absolute. What we know and find out should only ever be a stepping stone to the next question. The moment we assume that we have complete knowledge, we become dangerous communicators.

We hope this book will support you on your journey to becoming a more effective international communicator. We hope that it will encourage you to speak and to listen to others more thoughtfully, and that it will help you to understand and be understood better as you work internationally.

REFERENCES

2 Speaking

Turn taking: see Richard Lewis, *When Cultures Collide: Managing Successfully Across Cultures*, (London: Nicholas Brealey Publishing, 1996). See also Trompenaars, Alfons, Hampden-Turner, Charles and Trompenaars, Fons, *Riding the Waves of Culture: Understanding Diversity in Global Business*, (New York: McGraw-Hill Intercultural Assessment project (INCA), 1997). – www.incaproject.org/framework.htm

5 Building relationships

Relationship Awareness Theory: developed by Elias Porter, psychologist (1914–87). See for example: E.H. Porter, *Relationship Awareness Theory, Manual of Administration and Interpretation*, ninth edition. (Carlsbad, CA: Personal Strengths Publishing, Inc. 1973, 1996).

Communication and gender: Deborah Tannen, Professor of Linguistics at Georgetown University, USA. See for example: D. Tannen, *Gender and Discourse* (Oxford: Oxford University Press, 1966).

Relationship-building skills: Centre for Intercultural Learning at the Canadian Foreign Service Institute – www.intercultures.ca/cil-cai/overview-apercu-eng.asp?iso=ca

6 Networking

Conversation and group dynamics: see Ivan Misner, David Alexander, Brian Hilliard, *Networking Like a Pro: Turning Connections Into Contacts*, (California: Entrepreneur Media, 2009).

7 Building trust

Trust: Worldwork is a London-based agency responsible for developing The International Profiler (TIP), a questionnaire and feedback tool that has been developed to help managers and professionals understand where they put the behavioural emphasis when working internationally – www.worldwork.biz

8 Making decisions

Decision-making styles: A. Rowe and J. Boulgarides, *Managerial Decision Making: A Guide to Successful Business Decisions*, (New York: MacMillan, 1992).

11 Managing conflict

Stages of team development: Bruce W. Tuckman and Mary Ann C. Jensen, 'Stages of small group development revisited', *Group and Organizational Studies*, 2, (1977) 419–427.

Profiling team members: Myers-Briggs Type Indicator® (MBTI) – www.cpp.com/products/mbti/index.aspx

Profiling team members: Team Management Systems and the Team Management Wheel® of TMS Development International Ltd (TMSDI®) – www.tmsdi.com

READING LIST

This list contains one or two follow-up titles for further reading for most chapters of this book. If you are interested in learning more about the competences you need for working effectively across cultures, then you should read:

Jeremy Comfort and Peter Franklin, *The Mindful International Manager* (Kogan Page, 978-0-749461-97-3).

2 Speaking
Ron Scollon and Suzanne Wong Scollon, *Intercultural Communication: A Discourse Approach* (Blackwell, 978-0-631-22418-1).

Owen Hargie, *Skilled Interpersonal Communication: Research, Theory and Practice* (Routledge, 978-0-415-43204-7).

3 Listening
Nancy Kline, *Time to Think* (Cassell Illustrated, 978-0-706377-45-3).

Mark Brady, *The Wisdom of Listening* (Wisdom Publications, 978-0-861713-55-4).

5 Building relationships
Jerry Richardson, *The Magic of Rapport* (Meta Publications, 978-0-916990-44-2).

Deborah Tannen, *You Just Don't Understand: Women and Men in Conversation* (HarperCollins, 978-0-060959-62-3).

6 Networking
Ivan Misner, David Alexander and Brian Hilliard, *Networking Like a Pro: Turning Connections Into Contacts* (Entrepreneur Press, 978-1-59918-356-5).

Rob Yeung, *Networking: The New Rules* (Marshall Cavendish, 978-1-905736-30-0).

7 Building trust

C. Burke et al., *Trust in Leadership: A Multi-level Review and Integration* (The Leadership Quarterly, 2007) 606–632.

Ivana Marková and Alex Gillespie (eds), *Trust and Distrust: Sociocultural Perspectives* (Information Age Publishing, 978-1-59311-841-9).

8 Making decisions

Scott Plous, *The Psychology of Judgement and Decision-Making* (McGraw-Hill, 978-0-070504-77-6).

9 Influencing

Robert B. Cialdini, *Influence: The Psychology of Persuasion* (Collins, 978-0-061241-89-5).

Joseph O'Connor, *Leading With NLP: Essential Leadership Skills for Influencing and Managing People* (Thorsons, 978-0-722537-67-1).

10 Dealing with 'difficult people'

Robert M. Bramson, *Coping with Difficult People* (Dell, 978-0-440-20201-1).

11 Managing conflict

Roy J. Lewicki, Bruce Barry and David Saunders, *Negotiation: Readings, Exercises and Cases* (Irwin Professional, 978-0-07353-0314).

Max A. Eggert and Wendy Falzon, *The Resolving Conflict Pocketbook* (Management Pocketbooks, 978-1-903776-06-3).

12 Giving and getting feedback

Clive Fletcher, *Appraisal, Feedback and Development: Making Performance Review Work* (Routledge, 978-0-415-44691-4).

Joseph R. Folkman, *The Power of Feedback: 35 Principles for Turning Feedback from Others into Personal and Professional Change* (John Wiley, 978-0-471-99820-4).

13 Writing email: The basics

Paul Emmerson, *Email English* (Macmillan Education, 978-1-405-01294-2).

Nancy Flynn and Tom Flynn, *Writing Effective E-mail* (Kogan Page, 978-0-74943-326-0).

14 Writing email: Advanced
R. L. Trask, *How to Write Effective Emails* (Penguin, 978-0-14101-719-8).

Monica Seeley, *Brilliant Email: How to Win Back Time and Increase Your Productivity* (Pearson, 978-0-27374-255-5).

15 Telephoning
Susan Lowe, *Telephoning* (Delta Publishing, 978-1-900783-79-8).

Bob Dignen and Jon Dyson, *English for Telephoning (Business Minimax)* (York Associates, 978-1-900991-25-4).

16 Taking part in conference calls
Ida Shessel, *74 Tips for Absolutely Great Teleconference Meetings* (Multi-Media Publications, 978-1-895186-86-4).

Ken Taylor, *Fifty Ways to Improve your Telephoning and Teleconferencing Skills* (Summertown Publishing, 978-1-905992-06-5).

17 Working in virtual teams
Richard Lepsinger and Darleen DeRosa, *Virtual Team Success: A Practical Guide for Working and Leading from a Distance* (Pfeiffer, 978-0-470532-96-6).

Ian Fleming, *Virtual Teams Pocketbook* (Management Pocketbooks, 978-1-903776-41-4).

ANSWER KEY

Chapter 3

What stops us from listening effectively: Analysis

Our ability to listen is affected by three main factors, which are illustrated by what is going wrong in the three dialogues.

1 The message. In the first dialogue, the listener feels that this is not a relevant message. In the second dialogue, the listener is confused by the complexity of the explanation.

2 The speaker. Speakers whose tempo, volume or level of emotion is disturbing for the listener will find it more difficult to get their message across. Some listeners may also pay less attention if the speaker lacks status. This is a factor in the third dialogue, in which the listener wants to involve the team leader rather than waste time discussing a subject with a speaker who is not seen as having responsibility for the issue.

3 The listener. The greatest threat to effective listening is actually the listener. Listeners distort and reject messages in ways that they may not be conscious of. This happens particularly when the speaker's message is seen as a form of criticism or threat, or when the listener is under time pressure (as in the first dialogue). Listeners often undervalue the importance of what is said. As a result, they may lose the respect of the speaker: *Hey, he's not listening to me. Who does he think he is?* Also, the listener's ability to see things in new ways and to learn will be reduced.

Chapter 5

Lunch for two: Small talk strategies to get the conversation going – feedback

Jean takes the initiative (an important strategy) and asks an opening question (work is a safe topic). She is then quick to follow up with another question that shows some knowledge of the other person's working life. Sam recognises that the questions are not really information-oriented and so keeps his answers short before respectfully handing the conversation back to Jean by returning the question (*How about your work?*). Sam listens actively and positively; he repeats words Jean uses (*Finished?*) and shows empathy (*I can imagine.*) He also introduces a little humour to spice up the conversation (*…we'll have to find you something else to keep you busy*), to keep things light and friendly, and to indicate that the conversation topic is over and that it is time to order. Jean responds positively to the humour with an ironic comment (*… thanks very much for that thought*) and is sensitive to the fact that it is time to order.

Summary of strategies for building relationships at first meetings
- Taking the initiative
- Asking a question
- Asking a follow-up question
- Showing knowledge of the other person's working life
- Keeping answers short
- Handing the conversation back by returning a question
- Active and positive listening
- Repeating words which others use
- Showing empathy
- Introducing humour
- Responding to the humour of others positively
- Being sensitive to the need to order (specific to being in a restaurant)

Chapter 6

Conversation and group dynamics: An answer

B is the most obvious cluster to approach as the body language from both individuals looks open to a person joining. Cluster A seems locked in a strong conversation. In cluster C, the person on the bottom left of the three may be open to an approach as the body language indicates some awareness of a person entering from the doorway. Person E looks to be walking towards person D but it is not clear if these two people are open to a third person joining as they may know each other and so may be about to start a private conversation.

Chapter 8

Stages in an introduction to a meeting: Answer

Initiate: *OK, shall we get started?*

Welcome: *Firstly, a quick welcome to Jan, who has joined us from the Belgian office. Nice to have you here.*

Role: *Jan will be presenting some figures later when we talk about the new cross-border initiative.*

Agenda: *OK, in terms of agenda, if you all have it in front of you, as you can see, the main objective today is to take a decision on the next phase of the project. Do we feel ready to start, and, if so, when? We'll do an update of progress so far, that's from me. Then I just want to give you some information from the recent leadership meeting in Milan. And then we can talk about the decision and the pros and cons of moving on with things now or waiting.*

Rules: *Just to remind you of a few rules, as always: mobile phones off, and the native English speakers should try to speak clearly so that our colleagues from around the world can understand.*

Confirm: *OK?*

Begin: *Good, then let's get started with …*

Chapter 10

Test: How impatient are you? Comments

38–50: Your impatience is likely to be causing you and others problems. Try getting feedback from your boss and colleagues about this so that you realise the consequences of your behaviour. Then think seriously about implementing techniques for stronger emotional control.

25–37: You may be in control most of the time, but occasionally you are not operating effectively because your emotions are out of control. Try implementing the ideas in this unit for those situations in which you feel impatience may be a problem.

12–24: You are generally calm and collected. Think about how you can spread your calm to other team members to create a more productive atmosphere.

0–11: You are exceptional! If you know how you do this, then tell your colleagues. They will benefit.

Chapter 14

A task-oriented email: Model answer

There is no single correct answer to this question. In the model below, Jackie focuses purely on asking the main question and giving clear (solution-oriented) advice.

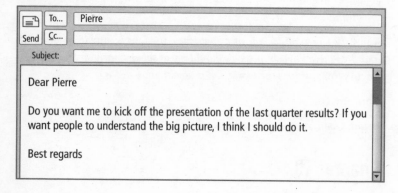

	To...	Pierre
Send	Cc...	
	Subject:	

Dear Pierre

Do you want me to kick off the presentation of the last quarter results? If you want people to understand the big picture, I think I should do it.

Best regards